ONE NATION, FIFTY STATES

by Imogene Forte

Incentive Publications, Inc.
Nashville, Tennessee

In order to make ONE NATION, FIFTY STATES a timely work to capture and hold students' attention, information was collected from a wide variety of sources, including reference works, brochures, materials developed by individual departments of tourism, chambers of commerce, and other original compilations. All information used in this work was diligently checked by our editorial department for accuracy insofar as possible. A consistent effort was maintained, however, to include folklore and cultural highlights as well as facts and statistics in order to present a mosaic comprised of fifty states, each contributing in its own unique way to one rich and diverse nation.

The publisher wishes to acknowledge and express appreciation for the cooperation and support of state agencies and associations responding to requests for current information.

Cover and illustrations by Cheryl Mendenhall
Edited by Jan Keeling

ISBN 0-86530-242-1

TABLE OF CONTENTS

PREFACE

A vital component of multicultural awareness is knowledge of one's own culture. Sadly, studies suggest that many students lack knowledge of their own country's history, geography, facts, folklore, and current events. Today's teachers want students to be prepared to take their places in the world with pride, with awareness of cultures around the world and close to home, and with a knowledge base that allows them to function effectively as citizens of a global society.

A **Whole Social Studies** approach to classroom instruction, using Social Studies as the focus for interdisciplinary units, can turn what first appears to be an insurmountable challenge into a golden opportunity for learning. This sensible strategy for integrating content areas, teaching basic skills, and maintaining high student interest levels is the foundation for this book.

One Nation, Fifty States was written with excitement and enthusiasm to fill teachers' expressed needs for a special kind of work: a collection of lively content-based activities that enable students to acquire a background knowledge of the United States and to develop appreciation of their rich and diverse heritage. While processing states and capitals, geographical locations, and historical and economic facts provides kids with the ready reference bank needed for future studies, it is the open-ended activities encompassed within the fifty units that provide intellectual challenges and provoke the use of higher-level thinking skills. This multidisciplinary approach cuts across content areas and highlights enrichment and creative activities in a manner designed to stimulate the quest for knowledge and further investigation.

A distinguishing feature of *One Nation, Fifty States* is that everything the student needs to complete the activities is right here between the pages of this book. The facts included were selected to be of high interest to children. Additional references may be used to enhance and extend the lessons, but they are not essential for completion of the activities. The states are arranged by region, with an alphabetical listing for easy reference. Each state's section begins with an outline map with labeled illustrations of the state flower, bird, and tree. Also included is a "Fast Fact Sheet" providing information such as the state capital, list of bordering states, nickname, and geographical, historical, and economic facts of importance. A "Unit-At-A-Glance" page presents lessons, activities, and projects in the areas of Language, Math, Environmental Studies, and Enrichment. Finally, a reproducible "Check-Up" worksheet, sometimes a puzzle, game, or quiz, provides a fun-and-easy yet sound method for teacher evaluation and/or student self-assessment.

A Bonus section includes teaching aids, helpful lists, additional maps for evaluation, individual worksheets, reproducible activity pages, an answer key for puzzles and quizzes found throughout the book, and a comprehensive index.

ALPHABETICAL LISTING OF STATES

STATE	CAPITAL	ABBREVIATIONS		PAGE
Alabama	Montgomery	AL	Ala.	59
Alaska	Juneau	AK		219
Arizona	Phoenix	AZ	Ariz.	161
Arkansas	Little Rock	AR	Ark.	63
California	Sacramento	CA	Calif.	205
Colorado	Denver	CO	Colo.	179
Connecticut	Hartford	CT	Conn.	11
Delaware	Dover	DE	Del.	37
Florida	Tallahassee	FL	Fla.	67
Georgia	Atlanta	GA	Ga.	71
Hawaii	Honolulu	HI		223
Idaho	Boise	ID	Ida.	183
Illinois	Springfield	IL	Ill.	109
Indiana	Indianapolis	IN	Ind.	113
Iowa	Des Moines	IA	Ia.	131
Kansas	Topeka	KS	Kans.	135
Kentucky	Frankfort	KY	Ky.	75
Louisiana	Baton Rouge	LA	La.	79
Maine	Augusta	ME	Me.	15
Maryland	Annapolis	MD	Md.	41
Massachusetts	Boston	MA	Mass.	19
Michigan	Lansing	MI	Mich.	117
Minnesota	St. Paul	MN	Minn.	139
Mississippi	Jackson	MS	Miss.	83
Missouri	Jefferson City	MO	Mo.	143
Montana	Helena	MT	Mont.	187
Nebraska	Lincoln	NE	Nebr.	147
Nevada	Carson City	NV	Nev.	191
New Hampshire	Concord	NH	N.H.	23
New Jersey	Trenton	NJ	N.J.	45
New Mexico	Santa Fe	NM	N. Mex.	165
New York	Albany	Ny	N.Y.	49
North Carolina	Raleigh	NC	N.C.	87
North Dakota	Bismarck	ND	N. Dak.	151
Ohio	Columbus	OH	O.	121
Oklahoma	Oklahoma City	OK	Okla.	169
Oregon	Salem	OR	Ore.	209
Pennsylvania	Harrisburg	PA	Pa.	53
Rhode Island	Providence	RI	R.I.	27
South Carolina	Columbia	SC	S.C.	91
South Dakota	Pierre	SD	S. Dak.	155
Tennessee	Nashville	TN	Tenn.	95
Texas	Austin	TX	Tex.	173
Utah	Salt Lake City	UT	Ut.	195
Vermont	Montpelier	VT	Vt.	31
Virginia	Richmond	VA	Va.	99
Washington	Olympia	WA	Wash.	213
West Virginia	Charleston	WV	W. Va.	103
Wisconsin	Madison	WI	Wis.	125
Wyoming	Cheyenne	WY	Wyo.	199

New England

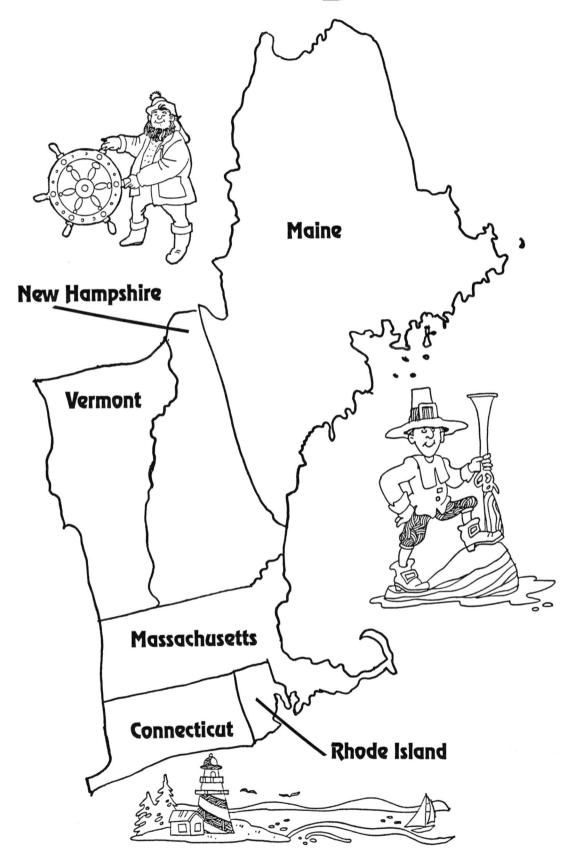

Maine

New Hampshire

Vermont

Massachusetts

Connecticut

Rhode Island

CONNECTICUT

The Constitution State

Mountain Laurel

White Oak

CONNECTICUT

Fact • Sheet

1. **CAPITAL:** Hartford

2. **BORDERING STATES:** New York, Massachusetts, Rhode Island

3. **THREE MAJOR CITIES:** Bridgeport • Hartford • New Haven

4. **ADMITTED TO UNION:** January 9, 1788

OTHER INTERESTING FACTS:

1. You may know that Connecticut is a Native American Indian name, but do you know what it means? It comes from a word that means "long tidal river." This long river (over 400 miles long) is the Connecticut River, the longest river in New England. It begins in New Hampshire, runs through Massachusetts, then runs right through the middle of Connecticut, ending up in Long Island Sound. In its valley grow vegetables and other crops—including tobacco, that crop that we may think only grows in the South!

2. Outside of the river valley, however, it is difficult to grow crops because the soil is hard and rocky. Early settlers of Connecticut could not rely on agriculture to support them. They became a seafaring people, building ships and using them for trade. They also became manufacturers, and supplied peddlers who traveled the country with their packs full of pins, hats, tin cups, combs, clocks, and brass kettles. One state nickname, "The Nutmeg State," arose because of the practices of some of these peddlers, who sold false nutmeg carved out of wood to unsuspecting customers! Most people of Connecticut undoubtedly prefer the nickname "The Constitution State."

3. Many of the products the Yankee peddlers sold were metal products, and, true to this heritage, most of today's factory workers in Connecticut make metal products (guns, silverware, helicopters, submarines, etc.). There is also a flavor of the past in the appearance of much of the state, with its old, well-kept white houses, little churches, and village greens.

SUPER FACT: *Did you know* that Connecticut has *another* nickname—"The Gadget State"? People in Connecticut made the first copper coins, the first stone crusher, the first American steel fishhook, and the first submarine torpedo boat.

Unit•At•A•Glance

Read and complete all activities, beginning with **I** and ending with **V**.

I. Language

Find and list as many words as you can using the letters in "Connecticut." Use each letter only as many times as it is used in the word. Try for at least sixteen words.

II. Environmental Studies

List at least ten items that Yankee peddlers may have carried in their packs to sell to householders on the trek across the country. Beside each item write the name of a modern-day item that could be substituted for the same item. If the same item is used today, make up a story and write it down.

III. Math

Using your Connecticut word list from Activity I, give yourself two points for every two-letter word, three points for every three-letter word, five points for every five-letter word, and ten points for every word with more than five letters. Total your score and then add a bonus point for every word with double letters. If your total score is more than 60, give yourself a bonus of ten points. If not, subtract a penalty of five points.

IV. Enrichment

Draw or paint a sequence of pictures showing the steps in building a ship in Connecticut, from the beginning of construction to launching.

V. Evaluation

Complete the "Connecticut Check-Up" worksheet.

CONNECTICUT

Check • Up

Pretend that you have been given the job of approving sketches for an informative factual brochure on the state of Connecticut. You notice that the artist became a little confused and added some sketches that had been done for another state.

Label the pictures with the correct words or phrases from the list below. Draw a box around each correctly-labeled item so it is ready for the brochure. Draw an "X" through each item that does not belong.

Word List:
Mountain Laurel   Robin   Yankee peddler
White Oak   shipbuilding

MAINE

The Pine Tree State

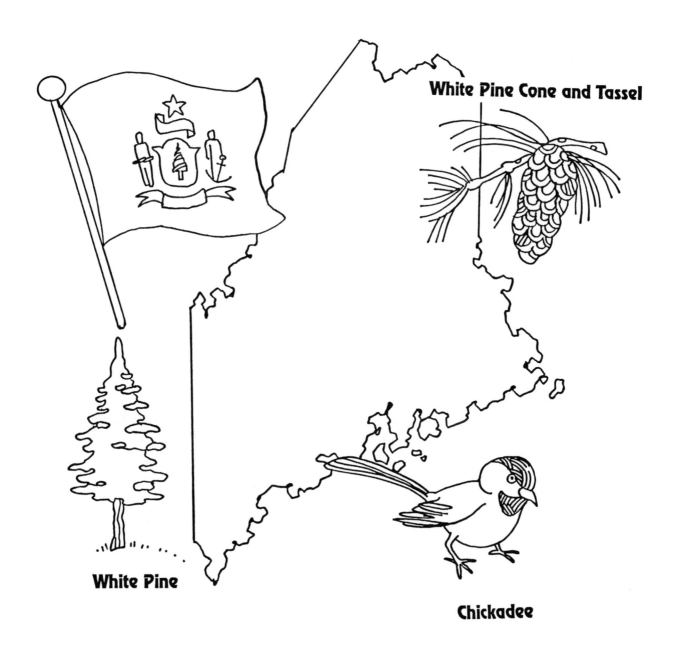

White Pine Cone and Tassel

White Pine

Chickadee

MAINE

Fact • Sheet

─ **FAST FACTS** ─

1. **CAPITAL:** Augusta

2. **BORDERING STATES:** New Hampshire

3. **THREE MAJOR CITIES:** Portland • Lewiston • Bangor

4. **ADMITTED TO UNION:** March 15, 1820

OTHER INTERESTING FACTS:

1. When you think of Maine, what comes to mind? The seashore? Picturesque old towns by the sea? A delightful place to visit in the summer with its cool ocean breezes and fresh air? In fact, Maine is largely forest; nine tenths of its land is covered with evergreens and deciduous trees. It has a greater percentage of forestland than does any other state in the Union.

2. Trees supply the material for logging, Maine's most important industry. For over three centuries, loggers have braved below-freezing temperatures to cut down trees and carry them out of the forest. For many years, loggers would pile the trees next to frozen rivers. When the rivers thawed in spring, the logs would be driven downstream. Today, logging companies use trucks to carry the logs to mills and factories.

3. Fishermen set out from the Maine coastline to fish for herring, cod, haddock, and scallops, and lobstermen set their traps. On the tidal flats, diggers look for clams and marine worms. These worms are bought by sport fishermen.

SUPER FACT: *Did you know* that most of our bloodworms and sandworms come from Maine? These worms are the best kind of bait for saltwater sport fishing. They are shipped as far as California.

Unit•At•A•Glance

Read and complete all activities, beginning with **I** and ending with **V**.

I. Language

Paint or draw a picture to show the image that each of the phrases below brings to your mind. Then write two Maine word images of your own and illustrate them.
• Icicles, icy, shiny, silvery, slippery, and cylindrical.

• Snow, white, sparkling, clean, covering the school, post office, and lamp posts.
• Tall evergreens, raising their boughs to the sky.
• Summer sunset, vivid, many-hued, fading softly to shed kindly light on rooftops, trees, and winding lanes.
• Marvelous, majestic, mystical, and mighty sailing ship, homeward bound to Maine.

II. Environmental Studies

Describe in a brief paragraph the industry or natural resource of Maine that is most impressive to you. Write another paragraph supporting your choice.

III. Math

Draw a dot-to-dot picture of a tall sailing ship or a Maine fishing boat, numbering the dots with consecutive odd integers.

IV. Enrichment

Plan a six-day vacation in Maine for your family. Choose the time of year you want to go, the recreation for your whole family, lodging, scenic and historical sites to be visited, and other points of interest to you.

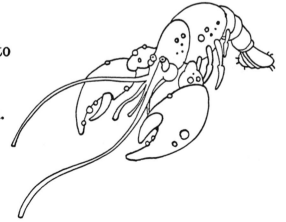

V. Evaluation

Complete the "Maine Check-Up" worksheet.

MAINE

Check • Up

Test your memory! Without referring to your Maine Fact Sheet or to any other reference material, use words from the word list at the bottom of the page to fill in the blanks in the sentences below. After you have completed the activity, use your reference materials to check your answers and to find answers for the ones you "didn't remember."

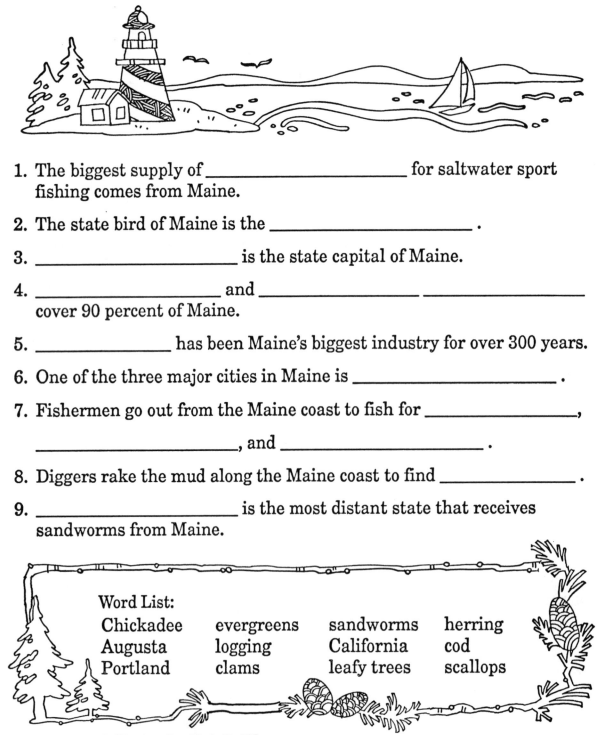

1. The biggest supply of _____ for saltwater sport fishing comes from Maine.

2. The state bird of Maine is the _____ .

3. _____ is the state capital of Maine.

4. _____ and _____ _____ cover 90 percent of Maine.

5. _____ has been Maine's biggest industry for over 300 years.

6. One of the three major cities in Maine is _____ .

7. Fishermen go out from the Maine coast to fish for _____, _____, and _____ .

8. Diggers rake the mud along the Maine coast to find _____ .

9. _____ is the most distant state that receives sandworms from Maine.

Word List:

Chickadee	evergreens	sandworms	herring
Augusta	logging	California	cod
Portland	clams	leafy trees	scallops

MASSACHUSETTS

The Bay State

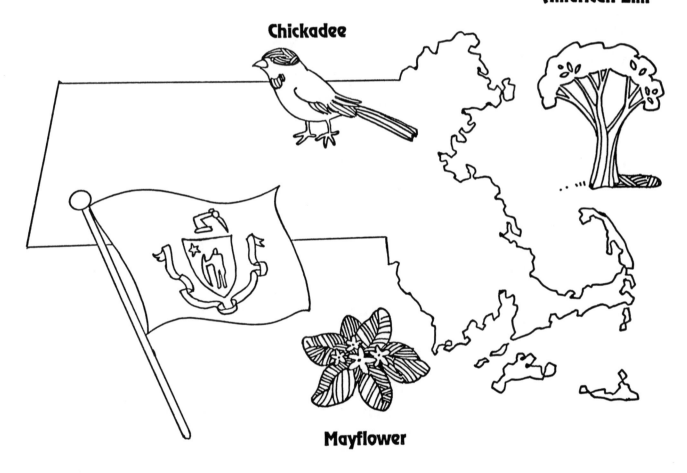

Chickadee

American Elm

Mayflower

MASSACHUSETTS

Fact • Sheet

FAST FACTS

1. **CAPITAL:** Boston

2. **BORDERING STATES:** New Hampshire, Vermont, New York, Connecticut, Rhode Island

3. **THREE MAJOR CITIES:** Boston • Worcester • Springfield

4. **ADMITTED TO UNION:** February 6, 1788

OTHER INTERESTING FACTS:

1. Travel to Boston and you'll feel close to America's past. There are actually red lines on the sidewalks, put there to mark landmarks of the American Revolution—take a tour of these landmarks, and you'll follow what is known as the "Freedom Trail." Farther from town are the battle-fields of Lexington and Concord. You can also see the oldest college in America, Harvard, which dates from 1636.

2. When you think of Cape Cod, do you think of a "vacation by the sea"? You might be shocked to learn that it began as a huge pile of rocks and sand, pushed southward by a glacier traveling from the north. Twelve thousand years ago the glacier melted. The remaining debris was shaped into the Cape by wind and weather and ocean, and plants and animals appeared. It was on the Cape's northernmost tip that the Pilgrims landed. They were headed for the gentler land of Virginia, but those hardy souls landed on the Cape, sailed to Plymouth, and managed to survive the rough climate of Massachusetts. Many people today love to travel to Cape Cod's sea cliffs and dune-covered beaches.

3. There are farms in the western areas of Massachusetts, and fine areas for hiking and camping. The town of Springfield has the armory that has been producing guns and ammunition for American soldiers ever since the time of George Washington. Dalton, Massachusetts, produces most of the paper that is used to make American dollar bills.

SUPER FACT: *Did you know* that the first game of basketball was played in 1891 at a Springfield YMCA school? Basketball's inventor, James Naismith, tacked real peach baskets to the walls. If a player "made a basket," someone had to climb up on a ladder to remove the ball!

Unit•At•A•Glance

Read and complete all activities, beginning with **I** and ending with **V.**

I. Language

Write a creative story based on one of the following story starters:
• My day on the Harvard campus . . .
• As our ship approached Plymouth Bay . . .
• A special Cape Cod memory . . .
• Historic Boston . . .

II. Environmental Studies

Pretend that you are a member of the United States Congress representing the people of Massachusetts. Select an issue of top concern you would have and draft a plan of action to address this concern for the betterment of your state during your term of office.

III. Math

Design a sand castle you would like to build on a long, lazy day on a Cape Cod beach. Establish the dimensions of your castle and estimate the amount of time it would take to build it.

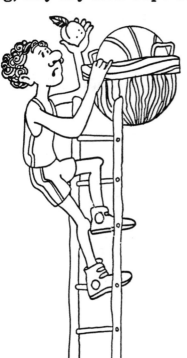

IV. Enrichment

To celebrate the birth of basketball in a Springfield, Massachusetts, gym in 1891, invent a new sport for people your age to play in a school gym. Develop rules for your game and give it a name.

V. Evaluation

Complete the "Massachusetts Check-Up" worksheet.

MASSACHUSETTS

Check • Up

Test your knowledge of Massachusetts by filling in the blanks in the sentences below using the words from the word list. Each word should be used only one time.

Word List:
Springfield   dollar bills   Cape Cod   Harvard
Bay State   Mayflower   glacier   Boston
Chickadee   Plymouth   basketball Freedom Trail

1. Red lines on the sidewalks in Boston mark the _____ _____ to landmarks of the American Revolution.

2. The oldest college in the United States, _____, is located in Boston.

3. _____ _____ is a well-known beach and resort area in Massachusetts. It was formed by a _____ almost 12,000 years ago.

4. The _____ is the state flower of Massachusetts.

5. People sometimes refer to Massachusetts as the _____ _____.

6. The sport of _____ was born in 1891 in Springfield, Massachusetts.

7. The pilgrims sailed to _____ after first landing on Cape Cod.

8. _____ is the capital of Massachusetts;_____ is one of its three major cities.

9. The _____ is the Massachusetts state bird.

10. Dalton, Massachusetts, makes most of the paper for our _____ _____ .

NEW HAMPSHIRE

The Granite State

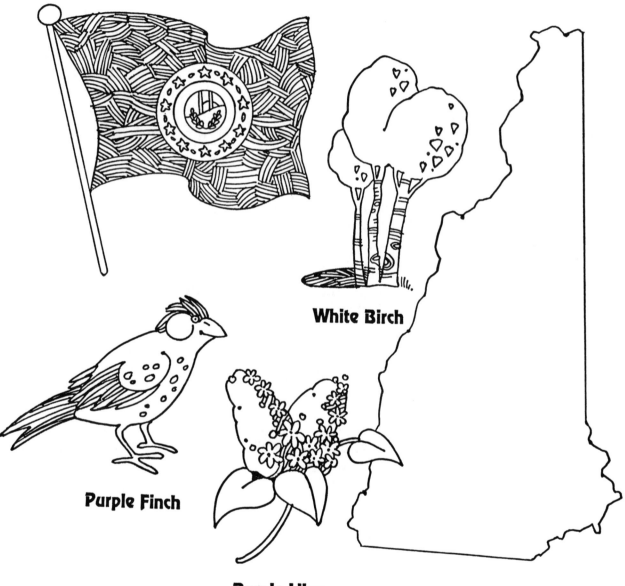

White Birch

Purple Finch

Purple Lilac

NEW HAMPSHIRE

Fact • Sheet

FAST FACTS

1. **CAPITAL:** Concord

2. **BORDERING STATES:** Vermont, Massachusetts, Maine

3. **THREE MAJOR CITIES:** Manchester • Nashua • Concord

4. **ADMITTED TO UNION:** June 21, 1788

OTHER INTERESTING FACTS:

1. New Hampshire's first-in-the-nation Presidential primary election every four years draws international attention and has made the Granite State well-known throughout the world. No candidate has ever won the Presidency without first winning in New Hampshire. This has given rise to the conviction at home and abroad that New Hampshire is a microcosm of America.

2. Another nickname for New Hampshire is the "Playland of New England." Recreational opportunities abound: swimming, camping, hiking, boating, hunting, fishing, skiing, and snowmobiling. New Hampshire has 18 miles of coastline, more than 2,000 lakes and ponds, 40,000 miles of streams, and 182 mountains over 3,000 feet high. The ample water supply has also contributed to making New Hampshire one of America's most highly industrialized states. But even with all its industry, New Hampshire is heavily forested. More trees grow here now and more wild game live among them than did a century ago.

3. New Hampshire's official trademark is the "Old Man of the Mountains," or "Great Stone Face." This natural granite formation is forty feet tall and resembles the profile of an old man's face. Nathaniel Hawthorne made this unusual phenomenon famous by writing about it in his short story, "The Great Stone Face."

SUPER FACT: *Did you know* New Hampshire was one of the original 13 colonies?

Unit•At•A•Glance

Read and complete all activities, beginning with **I** and ending with **V**.

I. Language

In ten minutes or less, write as many words as you can that describe or tell about an important fact related to New Hampshire. Try to write the longest words possible. Count the number of syllables in each word and give yourself a score using the following guidelines:
* One point for one-syllable words
* Two points for two-syllable words
* Three points for three-syllable words
* Four points for four-syllable words

Try for at least 36 points!

II. Environmental Studies

Place in rank order each sport listed below in terms of its importance to tourism in New Hampshire (in your opinion), with 1 being most important and 8 being least important. Give reasons for your first and last choices.

____ hunting ____ snowmobiling ____ skiing ____ hiking

____ fishing ____ boating ____ camping ____ swimming

III. Math

Make a dot-to-dot drawing, using numerals from 1 to 51, to represent the state tree of New Hampshire. Have a friend follow the dots to complete the picture.

IV. Enrichment

On heavy drawing paper or tagboard, draw an outline map of the state of New Hampshire. Add as many features as possible to add interest. Color the map and cut it into jigsaw puzzle pieces. Place the pieces in an envelope and ask a friend to work the puzzle to learn more about New Hampshire.

V. Evaluation

Complete the "New Hampshire Check-Up" worksheet.

NEW HAMPSHIRE

Check•Up

Complete the New Hampshire poster using drawings, symbols, words, and phrases to promote the state in a "United States Poster Power" contest.

RHODE ISLAND

Little Rhody

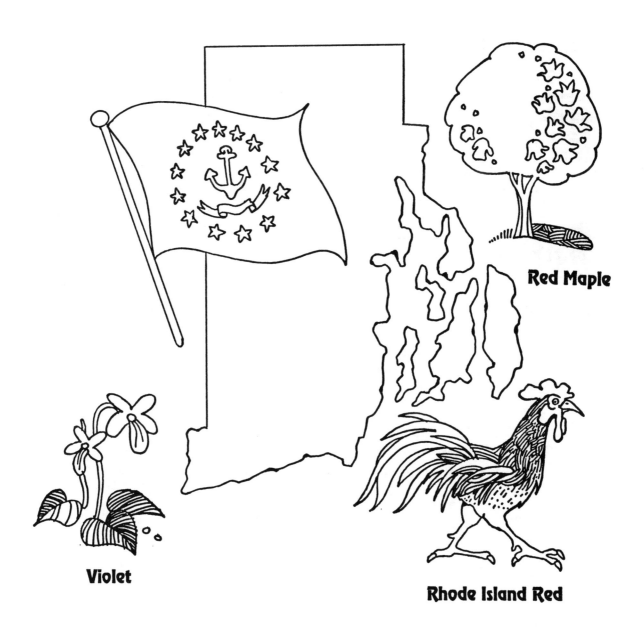

Red Maple

Violet

Rhode Island Red

RHODE ISLAND

Fact • Sheet

FAST FACTS

1. **CAPITAL:** Providence

2. **BORDERING STATES:** Massachusetts, Connecticut

3. **THREE MAJOR CITIES:** Providence • Warwick • Cranston

4. **ADMITTED TO UNION:** May 29, 1790

OTHER INTERESTING FACTS:

1. Rhode Island is the smallest state in the Union. Five hundred Rhode Islands would fit into the state of Alaska, the largest state. (However, the population of Rhode Island is twice that of Alaska.)

2. Providence, Rhode Island, was established by Roger Williams, who left Massachusetts and its oppressive religious rules. Williams felt that a person's religion was not the business of government, and his rules of government did not dictate anyone's religion. "Freedom of Religion" was to become one of the basic rights on which our country was founded.

3. Some of the oldest industries in the United States had their start in Rhode Island. The Old Slater Mill in Pawtucket, built in 1793, was the birthplace of the American factory system. It was a wooden mill with a bell tower, and in it cotton was machine-spun successfully for the first time.

SUPER FACT: *Did you know* that Pelham Street in Newport, Rhode Island, was the first street to be lit by gaslight? This was in 1806.

Unit•At•A•Glance

Read and complete all activities, beginning with **I** and ending with **V**.

I. Language

Pretend that you live in Rhode Island. Write journal entries for one week (7 days). List your activities at home, at school, and in the community.

II. Environmental Studies

Write a guide to be used by a group of senior citizens on a bus tour of Rhode Island. List scenic and historical spots to be visited, suggested stopovers, and recreational opportunities. Also suggest the best time of year for the tour.

III. Math

Using only the following geometrical shapes, design a collage to represent Rhode Island. Write a symbol or word in each shape to tell something about the state.

IV. Enrichment

Design a souvenir representative of Rhode Island. It will be presented by the tour company as a memento of the trip to the senior citizens group for whom you wrote the tour guide in Activity II.

V. Evaluation

Complete the "Rhode Island Check-Up" worksheet.

RHODE ISLAND

Check•Up

Make up a Rhode Island mini-trivia game.
Write questions about important facts related
to the state on the cards and answers on the
backs of the cards. Cut the cards apart and ask
a friend to play the game with you.

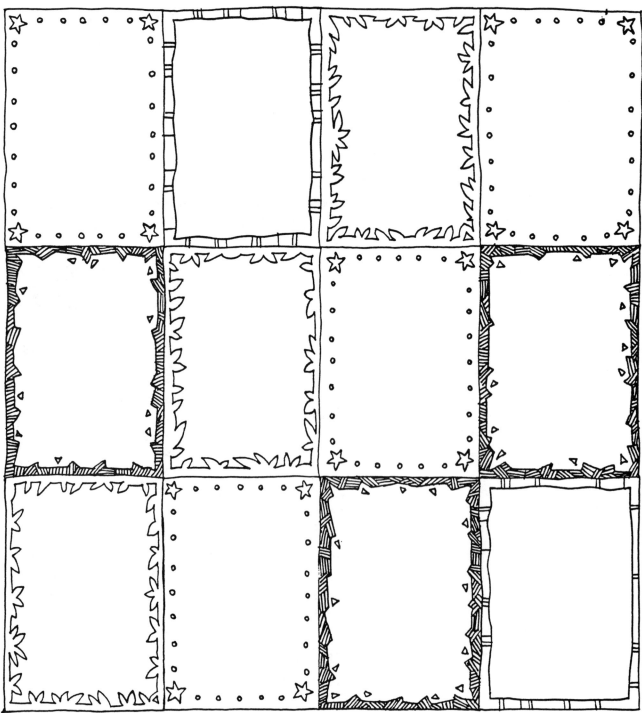

VERMONT

The Green Mountain State

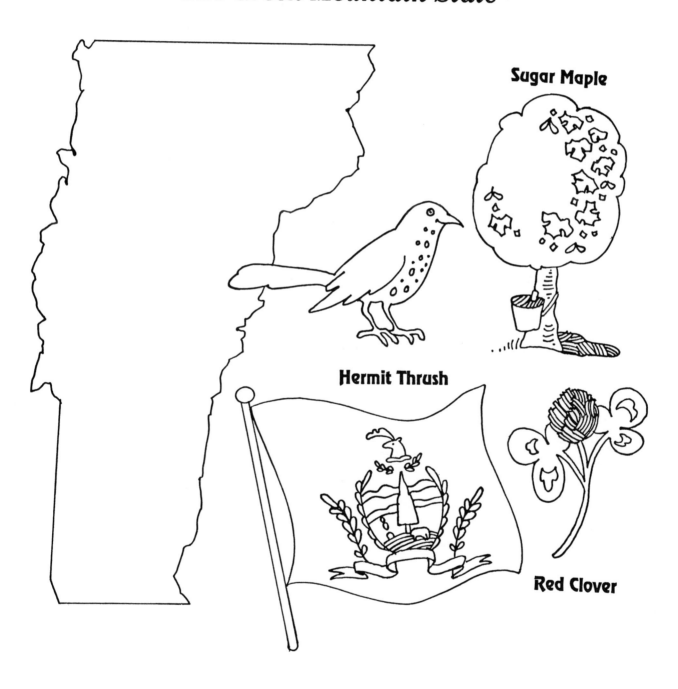

Sugar Maple

Hermit Thrush

Red Clover

VERMONT

Fact • Sheet

─── FAST FACTS ───

1. **CAPITAL:** Montpelier

2. **BORDERING STATES:** New York, Massachusetts, New Hampshire

3. **THREE MAJOR CITIES:** Burlington • Rutland • Bennington

4. **ADMITTED TO UNION:** March 4, 1791

OTHER INTERESTING FACTS:

1. Despite its nickname, "The Green Mountain State," for much of the year Vermont is the state of snow! There's an old saying about Vermont's weather: "Nine months snow and three months poor sledding"— and in some years, it's really true! In 1816, snow fell in July and August.

2. Vermont produces more maple syrup than does any other state. This activity is known as "sug'rin'." In late winter and early spring, sap is collected from maple trees through small spouts that are tapped into their trunks. The sap is then boiled in a sugarhouse for up to fifteen hours to make maple syrup. A grove of maple trees is called a "sugarbush."

3. The world's largest granite plant is in Barre, Vermont. Vermont also produces a lot of limestone and marble.

SUPER FACT: *Did you know* that the first chair lift in the East lifted skiers up Vermont's Mount Mansfield in 1940?

VERMONT

Unit•At•A•Glance

Read and complete all activities, beginning with **I** and ending with **V**.

I. Language

Write an original mystery story using one of
the following topics:
• The mysterious skier appeared out of nowhere . . .
• The first snowfall came more than a month early . . .
• First thunder, then lightning, then the dark . . .
• No one was prepared for the worst blizzard in history . . .

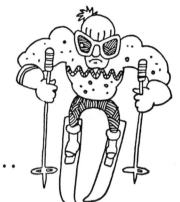

II. Environmental Studies

The first person to cross the entire United States by automobile was Dr. H.
Nelson Jackson, a Burlington, Vermont, physician, who started out in San
Francisco in 1903. Compare and contrast Dr. Jackson's trip across the
nation with an automobile trip from San Francisco to Vermont today.
Consider the type of automobile, time, lodging, cost, etc.

III. Math

"Pepper and salt, sugar and cream, bread and butter, Vermont maple syrup
and pancakes—what would one be without the other?" Here's a quick and
easy recipe for "Pancakes for One." Copy the recipe,
multiplying the ingredients by the number of people
in your family, so you'll be ready to serve up a super
Sunday pancake breakfast.

PANCAKES FOR ONE
• 1 egg white   • 1 egg yolk • ¼ cup cottage cheese
• pinch of salt   • 2 tablespoons flour

Beat the egg white. In a separate bowl, beat the yolk. Stir in
the salt, flour, and cottage cheese with the yolk; fold in the
white. Drop by spoonfuls onto a hot, lightly greased griddle.
Cook on both sides until golden brown. Serve at once with maple syrup.

IV. Enrichment

Design a winter sport suit to keep you warm on a Vermont
ski slope. Don't forget boots, hat, and mittens. Draw and
color yourself in the suit and add a snowy background.

V. Evaluation

Complete the "Vermont Check-Up" worksheet.

33

VERMONT

Design a bulletin board display for your school media center to acquaint students with facts and information about Vermont. Be as creative as you can and add ideas of your own to share your knowledge of the "Green Mountain State."

State Bird   State Flag

State Flower   Natural Resources

Mid-Atlantic States

New York

Pennsylvania

New Jersey

Delaware

Maryland

DELAWARE

The First State

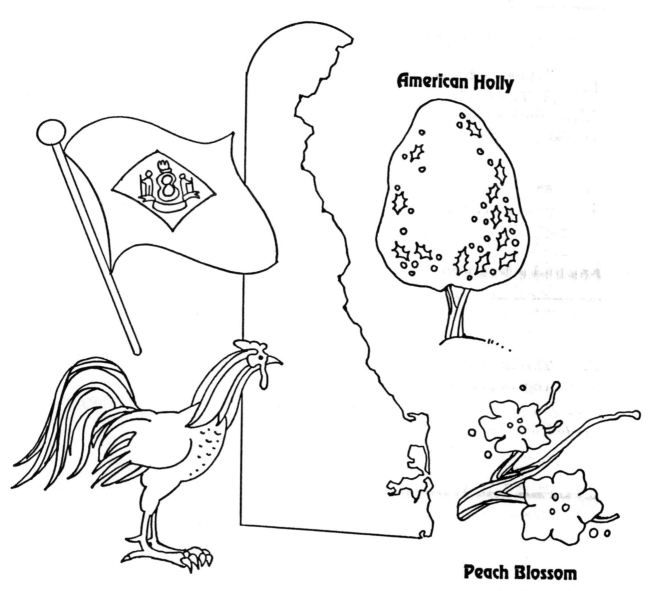

American Holly

Blue Hen Chicken

Peach Blossom

DELAWARE

Fact • Sheet

1. **CAPITAL:** Dover

2. **BORDERING STATES:** Maryland, Pennsylvania, New Jersey

3. **THREE MAJOR CITIES:** Wilmington • Newark • Dover

4. **ADMITTED TO UNION:** December 7, 1787

OTHER INTERESTING FACTS:

1. Delaware can well be called the U.S.A.'s number one state, or first state, since it was the first state to be admitted to the Union. Flags of three nations flew over the Delaware Bay Colony: first Dutch, then Swedish, and, finally, English, before the U.S. Constitution was approved.

2. The people of Delaware are very serious about their commitment to protection of natural wildlife. Strict laws have been enacted to save the seashore, and wildlife refuges have been established all along Delaware's beaches. Steel mills, oil refineries, and other ecology-threatening businesses are prohibited from constructing buildings within two miles of the coast. This is an especially daring move for this small state, since so much of its economy depends on manufacturing.

3. The DuPont Company is the largest chemical company in the world and has headquarters located in Delaware. We have the DuPont Company to thank for rayon, nylon, dacron, orlon, teflon, and many other synthetic materials.

SUPER FACT: *Did you know* Delaware is the only state that has a rounded border?

DELAWARE

Unit•At•A•Glance

Read and complete all activities, beginning with **I** and ending with **V**.

I. Language

List ten adjectives that describe Delaware. Underline the one that you think best describes this state. Explain the reasons for your choice.

II. Environmental Studies

Think about all that you have learned about Delaware. Name the one thing that you think makes the greatest contribution to the people of the nation as a whole. Write a paragraph explaining the importance of this contribution.

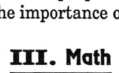

III. Math

Estimation is a very important skill. List three ways estimation skills can be used for tracking and learning about the habits of migrating birds in Delaware's wildlife refuges. For each way listed, tell what kind of history and factual records would be used to arrive at the estimate.

IV. Enrichment

Use the adjectives that you listed in the Language activity to develop a "feeling" poster to represent the state. Choose a crayon or marker whose color "matches" the word, then write the word in a style that "feels" right to you. When all the words are written, use scrolls, lines, and borders to finish off your poster.

V. Evaluation

Complete the "Delaware Check-Up" worksheet.

DELAWARE

Check•Up

Imagine that you have been awarded an all-expense-paid traveling vacation in Delaware for one week. There is no limit on the budget, means of transportation, or type of lodging. The only restrictions are that you must travel in a one-way direction, with no backtracking, and your trip must begin in one bordering state and end in another. Show your trip plan below.

Things to THINK ABOUT:
1. Will you stay in hotels, inns, or in people's homes? Why?
2. Which historic or scenic sites do you want to visit?
3. What do you want to learn about the people of Delaware?

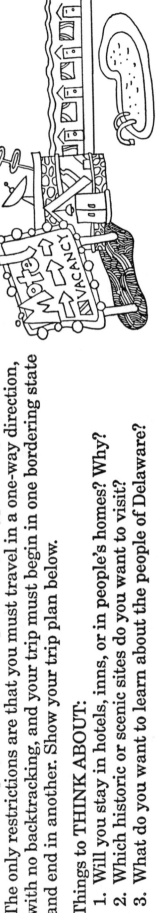

	Travel From (city)	Travel To (city)	Means Of Transportation	Things To See And Do
Day 1				
Day 2				
Day 3				
Day 4				
Day 5				
Day 6				
Day 7				

MARYLAND

The Old Line State

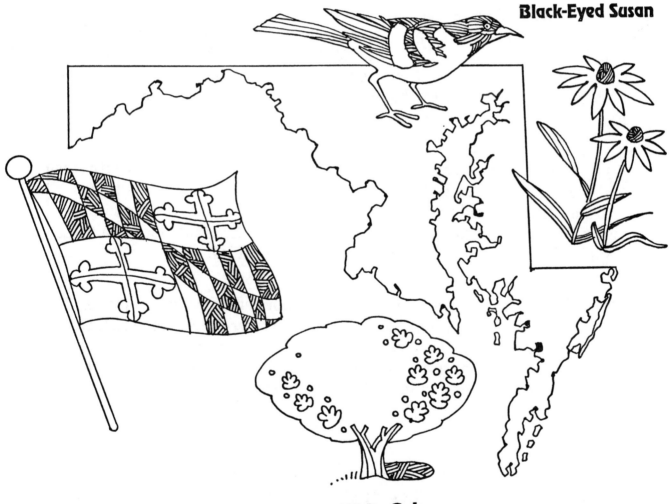

Baltimore Oriole

Black-Eyed Susan

White Oak

MARYLAND

Fact • Sheet

```
┌─────────────────────────────── FAST FACTS ───┐
│                                               │
│  1. CAPITAL: Annapolis                        │
│                                               │
│  2. BORDERING STATES: Pennsylvania, Delaware, Virginia, West │
│     Virginia                                  │
│                                               │
│  3. THREE MAJOR CITIES: Baltimore • Rockville • Bowie │
│                                               │
│  4. ADMITTED TO UNION: April 28, 1788         │
│                                               │
└───────────────────────────────────────────────┘
```

OTHER INTERESTING FACTS:

1. ❑ Maryland has seemed to be two states because its land mass was divided almost completely in two by the Chesapeake Bay. People who lived on one side of the Bay had little contact with those who lived on the other. In 1952, the world's longest all-steel bridge over salt water was built by Maryland, uniting the two Maryland groups, and opening up the Eastern Shore to new industries.

2. ❑ An estuary is a body of water where salty seawater mixes with fresh riverwater—and Chesapeake Bay is the nation's largest estuary! The tiny animals and underwater plants that live in this mix are food for bigger animals, fishes, oysters, crabs, and clams. Thus the "food chain" begins with microscopic life and ends up at our tables.

3. ❑ Chickens are raised on the eastern shore of Maryland, apples and peaches are grown in the central and western counties, and tobacco is grown in the south. One could say another huge "crop" is that of houses and apartments in the area around the District of Columbia. There has been a tremendous growth in population, and in the need for housing to accommodate it.

SUPER FACT: *Did you know* that the Maryland State House, built between 1772 and 1779, is the oldest state capitol still in continuous legislative use? From November 26, 1783, to August 13, 1784, it housed the Continental Congress. It is the only State House ever to have served as the nation's capitol.

Unit•At•A•Glance

Read and complete all activities, beginning with **I** and ending with **V**.

I. Language

Based on what you have learned about Maryland's food products, make up a festive five-course celebration menu for the holiday that you and your family most enjoy. Include your favorite foods. Put a star beside the foods which contain basic ingredients that could have come from Maryland.

II. Environmental Studies

Design four placemats to show what happens to Chesapeake Bay life that is destined for the dinner table. The first placemat should show steps in the natural food chain, the second placemat: acquisition of food, the third: food processing, and the fourth: the shipping of food products from the Chesapeake Bay to America's dinner tables.

III. Math

Make up five math word problems—
one using addition facts, one using subtraction facts, and three using multiplication facts—based on Maryland's seafood or agricultural products.

IV. Enrichment

Design a souvenir menu for your five-course holiday dinner. Add illustrations and color to make it a truly memorable keepsake.

V. Evaluation

Complete the "Maryland Check-up" worksheet.

MARYLAND

Check • Up

Write a factual report on Maryland's rich history, culture, natural resources, industries, state symbols, and other unique features. Write it as if you were contributing material to a Social Studies book for students your age.

NEW JERSEY

The Garden State

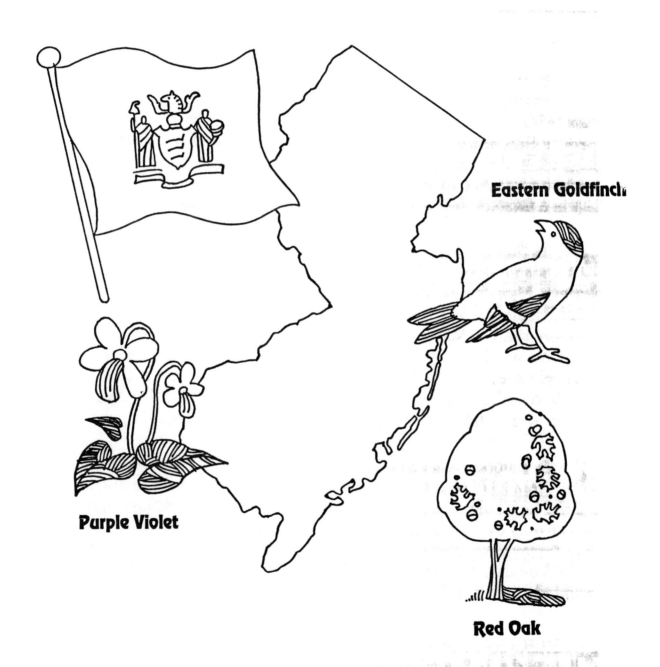

Eastern Goldfinch

Purple Violet

Red Oak

NEW JERSEY

Fact • Sheet

OTHER INTERESTING FACTS:

1. Have you always thought that New Jersey is completely covered with industry? Have you ever wondered why it's called The "Garden State"? New Jersey is called "The Garden State" because of its splendid gardens that contain almost every kind of flower and tree that you can think of. It also has 8,000 farms which produce most of the fresh summer produce consumed by people in New York City and Philadelphia. Atlantic City is a famous New Jersey resort and a popular vacation city.

2. To find the population density of an area, count the number of people living within a square mile. If you lived in the area around Newark, New Jersey, you might think you were living in a very crowded state! People live so close together in this area that in some places there are more than 50,000 people in a square mile. Move to the "Pine Barrens" near Chatworth, and you'll find a different story. In the Barrens live about 15 people per square mile, and houses are often so far apart that you'd have to travel a very long distance to see another person. Indeed, three fourths of the state is covered with forests and small farms.

3. In several research laboratories in New Jersey, during the period from 1875 to 1900, Thomas Alva Edison perfected the phonograph and the lightbulb, along with many other inventions. Edison's mind was not the only inventive one in the Garden State: other creative people in New Jersey developed the earliest experimental submarines, produced world-famous glassware, invented the solid body electric guitar, and invented grape juice!

SUPER FACT: *Did you know* that Atlantic City's boardwalk, made of fir planks, is five miles long?

NEW JERSEY

Read and complete all activities, beginning with **I** and ending with **V.**

I. Language

Write a three-minute speech for a
New Jersey spokesperson to deliver
to a group of tour company owners
to encourage them to plan weekend
tours to New Jersey resorts. Be sure
to point out opportunities for
sightseeing and recreation.

II. Environmental Studies

Pretend that you are a newly-arrived immigrant
from a non-English-speaking country and you are
just learning to speak English. Make a list of jobs
that might be available to you in New Jersey and
list the job skills needed for each.

III. Math

Make up three word problems related to New
Jersey's manufacturing industries and the use of
money. Ask a friend to solve your problems and
check the answers.

IV. Enrichment

Create a brand-new
item that might be
manufactured in

one of New Jersey's factories. Give your item
a name and a description. Create a newspaper or magazine ad to introduce your
product to the market.

V. Evaluation

Complete the "New Jersey Check-Up" worksheet.

NEW JERSEY

Check • Up

Use words from the word list below to complete the summary sheet for an
"All States Information Guide." Two of the words in the word list will not
be used.

Word List:

Eastern Gold Finch	residents	relaxation
Red Oak	farms	purple violet
populated	forests	The Garden State
diverse	produce	Cardinal
apart	Atlantic City	

In many areas, New Jersey is a heavily _____ state. In other
parts of the state, houses are far _____ and there are very few
_____. If you look at the crowded areas, it is hard to believe
that 75% of the state is made up of small _____ and
_____. Much of the fresh _____ eaten in New York City
and Philadelphia comes from New Jersey. Resorts like _____
_____ provide vacations and recreation for many hard-working
New Jersey residents.

New Jersey's nickname is _____ _____ _____. The state
flower is the _____ _____, the _____ _____ _____
is the state bird, and the _____ _____ is the state tree.

All in all, New Jersey is an interesting and _____ state.

NEW YORK

The Empire State

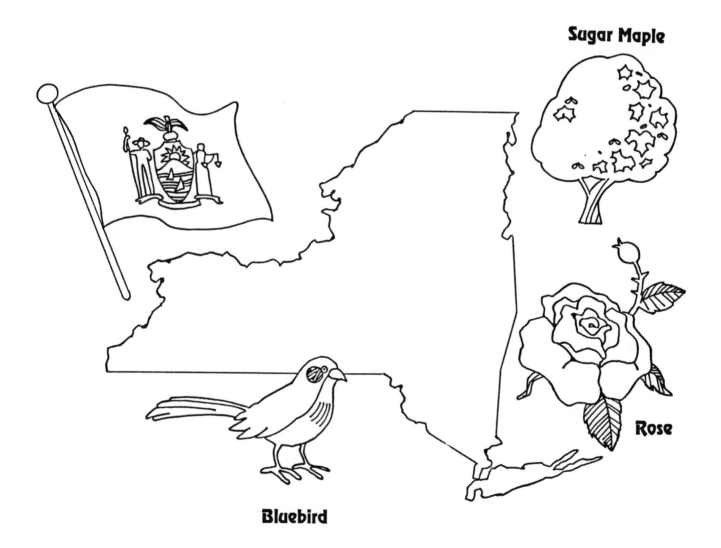

Sugar Maple

Rose

Bluebird

NEW YORK

Fact • Sheet

FAST FACTS

1. **CAPITAL:** Albany

2. **BORDERING STATES:** Pennsylvania, New Jersey, Connecticut, Massachusetts, Vermont

3. **THREE MAJOR CITIES:** New York City • Buffalo • Rochester

4. **ADMITTED TO UNION:** July 26, 1788

OTHER INTERESTING FACTS:

1. Why is New York called "The Empire State?" This name comes from a remark that George Washington once made. He called New York the "Seat of Empire," for he believed that the entire country would be run by the people of this state. New York is still a place of power. Located here are the New York Stock Exchange, important banks that deal in large sums of money, big television networks, and the headquarters of the United Nations.

2. New York State is first in manufacturing, and always has been. Water has been the major source of its energy. Streams powered flour mills and the first factories. Later, with the advent of hydroelectric power, water was used to generate electricity. The first North American use of hydroelectric power took place in New York.

3. Your mental image of New York may be one of an impressive skyline with skyscrapers and the Statue of Liberty. But two thirds of the state is forestland, mountains, meadows, and farms. North of New York City is Adirondack Park, the largest wilderness in the eastern United States. Some of the people who live in this wilderness live off the land, and some are guides or trappers. Some still live in log cabins the way people did long ago.

SUPER FACT: *Did you know* that New York City was the first capital of the United States? George Washington was inaugurated as first president in New York on April 30, 1789.

Unit•At•A•Glance

Read and complete all activities, beginning with **I** and ending with **V**.

I. Language

New York City has been called the most exciting city in the world. With Central Park, stage and musical shows, museums, ethnic communities, tall skyscrapers filled with businesses of every nature, the United Nations, shops and retail outlets from all over the world, and cultural and artistic communities richly representative of the arts and sciences, it is no surprise that New York City is one of the world's most visited cities. Make a list of at least twelve adjectives that could be used to describe New York City.

II. Environmental Studies

Make a daily plan, from 7:00 a.m. to 12:00 midnight, for how you would spend your time if you had only one day to spend in New York City. Where would you go, what would you see, and what would you do?

III. Math

Pretend that you have $100.00 to spend during your big day in New York City. Make a budget for the day, allotting money for food, transportation (subway, bus, or taxi), entertainment, and souvenirs. Remember, New York City is one of the most expensive cities in the world. Plan your expenditures carefully so that you are not caught penniless before the end of the day.

IV. Enrichment

Design a souvenir T-shirt that you would like to buy as a memento of your New York experience.

V. Evaluation

Complete the "New York Check-Up" worksheet.

NEW YORK

Check•Up

It is important to remember that, in addition to its famous city, New York State is made up of forests, mountains, parks, meadows, farmland, waterways, and manufacturing sites. To test your "New York Knowledge," in just five minutes try to write 25 important facts about New York State on the Fast Fact sheet below:

NEW YORK STATE FAST FACTS

_____

_____

_____

_____

_____

_____

_____

_____

_____

_____

_____

_____

_____

_____

_____

PENNSYLVANIA

The Keystone State

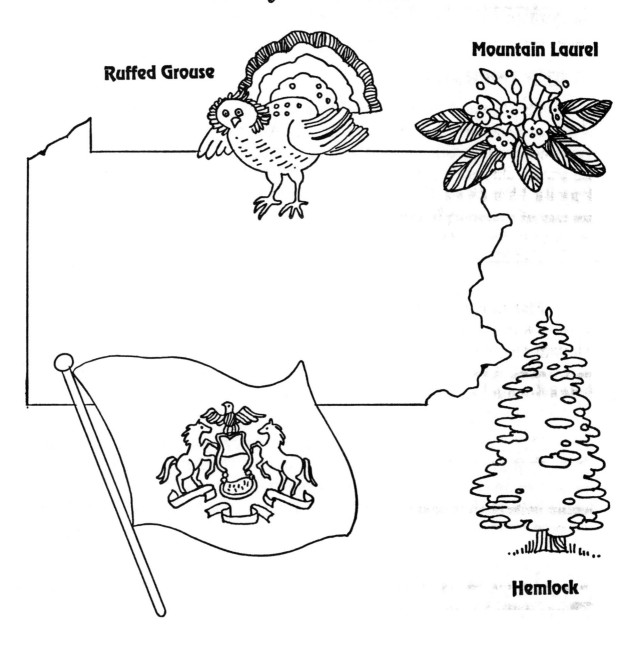

Ruffed Grouse

Mountain Laurel

Hemlock

PENNSYLVANIA

Fact • Sheet

─── FAST FACTS ───

1. **CAPITAL:** Harrisburg

2. **BORDERING STATES:** New York, New Jersey, Maryland, West Virginia, Ohio, Delaware

3. **THREE MAJOR CITIES:** Philadelphia • Pittsburgh • Erie

4. **ADMITTED TO UNION:** December 12, 1787

OTHER INTERESTING FACTS:

1. □ This large, 300-mile-wide state is home to a wide variety of people and places. It connects Northeast America with the Midwest. Its rivers carry ships that will distribute Pennsylvania products to the rest of the world. The state has good land for farms and is wealthy in mineral deposits. Two rivers, the Allegheny River and Monongahela River, meet at the city of Pittsburgh, famous for manufacturing steel. The two rivers join together to form the Ohio River. Ships that travel this river may end up in the Gulf of Mexico.

2. □ Pittsburgh was a natural city to become the "Steel City." Its surrounding hills produce tremendous amounts of the soft coal (bituminous coal) that is made into coke, which fuels the furnaces that make steel. Another mineral used in making steel is limestone, and Pennsylvania has huge limestone deposits.

3. □ There are almost 60,000 farms in Pennsylvania, producing crops that are worth almost 3 billion dollars. The Amish people own and operate some of the most valuable farms in the state. Since most Amish people believe that God does not want them to use electricity or cars, they live now much as they did a hundred years ago.

SUPER FACT: *Did you know* that the first working oil well in America was drilled in Pennsylvania (near Titusville) in 1859?

PENNSYLVANIA

Unit•At•A•Glance

Read and complete all activities, beginning with **I** and ending with **V**.

I. Language

Pretend you are planning a visit to
Pennsylvania. Make a list of three things
you want to see, three things you want to
do, and three things you want to find
out. Write a brief plan to enable you to achieve all your goals in three days.

II. Environmental Studies

Make a list of things people living in the
congested factory regions of Pennsylvania could
do to fight air, water, and land pollution.

III. Math

List from 1 to 9, in order of their importance to
you, the goals you named in Language Activity
#1. Make up three math word problems related
to the goals ranked 1, 2, and 3.

IV. Enrichment

Plan your wardrobe for a
three-day trip to
Pennsylvania. Make a
packing list to be sure
your bags are packed with
"all the right stuff."

V. Evaluation

Complete the
"Pennsylvania Check-Up"
worksheet.

PENNSYLVANIA

Check • Up

Write a journal entry for each of the three imaginary days you will spend in Pennsylvania. Tell what you will do, where you will stay, and what you will see or learn each day. Try to include specific cities, scenic sights, industries, the state symbols, and other interesting facts about the "Keystone State."

The South

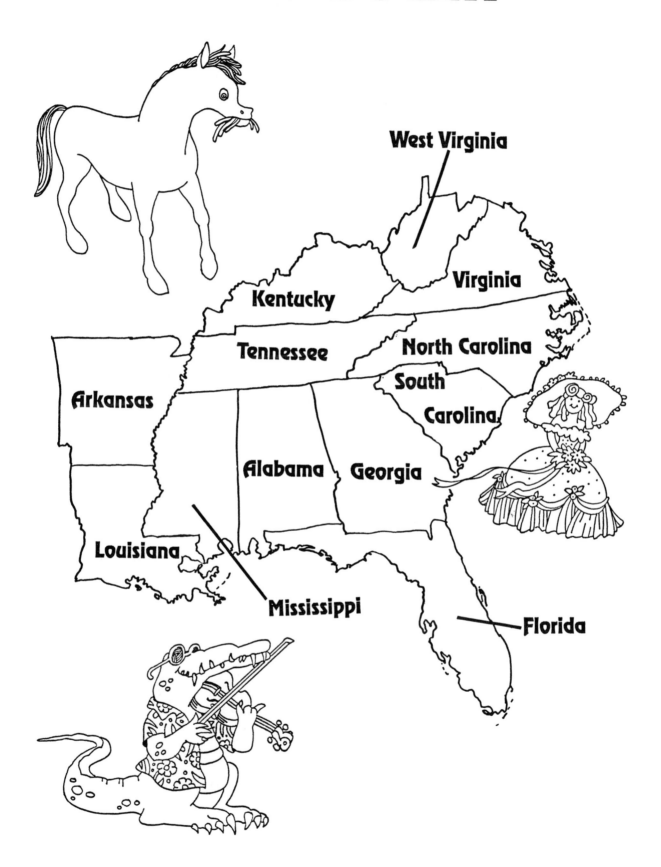

West Virginia

Virginia

Kentucky

Tennessee

North Carolina

South

Carolina

Arkansas

Alabama

Georgia

Louisiana

Mississippi

Florida

ALABAMA

The Heart Of Dixie

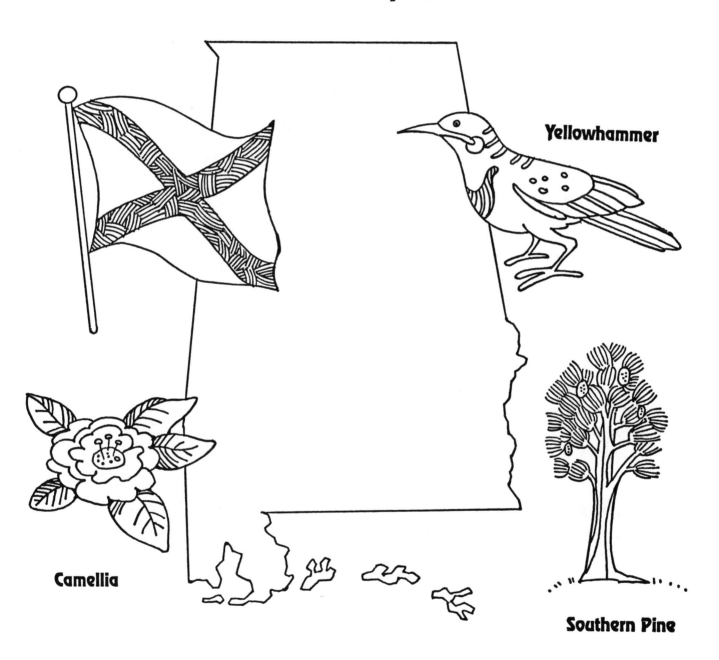

Yellowhammer

Camellia

Southern Pine

ALABAMA

Fact • Sheet

FAST FACTS

1. **CAPITAL:** Montgomery

2. **BORDERING STATES:** Mississippi, Tennessee, Georgia, Florida

3. **THREE MAJOR CITIES:** Birmingham • Mobile • Montgomery

4. **ADMITTED TO UNION:** December 14, 1819

OTHER INTERESTING FACTS:

1. For many years cotton was overwhelmingly the most important crop in Alabama. In the early 1900's a tiny bug called the boll weevil infested the cotton fields and destroyed them. Farmers were forced to begin growing other crops, including peanuts and vegetables, and to raise more hogs, cattle, and chickens. In time, many Alabamans became grateful that the ugly little bug had made it necessary for them to grow other profitable crops!

2. Alabama's Gulf Shores are dotted with fishing villages and with seaports that are havens for ships from many countries. Along these shores you will find shrimp boats and vacationing sunbathers. Seashore activities enrich Alabama's economy.

3. Because Alabama is rich in coal, limestone, natural gas, sand, gravel, clay, and iron ore, it has become a state of many industrial plants. Birmingham is a major center for steel mills and other heavy industry.

SUPER FACT: *Did you know* that Birmingham is sometimes called the "Pittsburgh of the South" because of its steel mills and heavy industries?

Unit•At•A•Glance

Read and complete all activities, beginning with **I** and ending with **V**.

I. Language

Create a word-find or crossword puzzle
using the following ten words, plus ten
others selected by you to represent facts
related to your study of Alabama: (1)
cotton (2) peanuts (3) Gulf Coast (4) steel
(5) shrimping (6) seaports (7) Birmingham (8) farming (9) Mobile (10) coal.

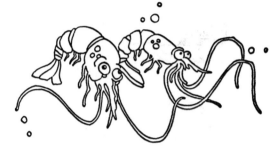

II. Environmental Studies

Look up and write definitions for hurricane, thunderstorm, squall, and
tide. Daily weather forecasts are important to people living on Alabama's
Gulf Coast. Tell why and how each of the following persons would depend
on daily weather forecasts to plan activities for the day:

- boat builder
- seafood buyer or processor
- ship captain
- commercial fisherman
- recreational facility owner

III. Math

Devise a brand-new never-before-thought-of recipe for a
treat using peanuts. Set yourself an ingredients budget with
a ten-dollar limit. Beside each ingredient write the estimated
cost. Determine how close you came to your budgeted limit by
adding up the cost of the ingredients (according to your
estimate) and subtracting the total from your budget figure.
If your estimated total can't be subtracted from the budget
figure, you're over budget! Try out your recipe if you dare.

IV. Enrichment

Fold a sheet of drawing paper in half. Now think about the pictures that
formed in your mind as you learned about the steel mills and other
factories in the city of Birmingham. Do the same thing with the pictures
brought to mind by the seaports and fishing villages which dot Alabama's
Gulf Shores. Draw or paint a picture on each half of your paper to show
your mental image. Give each picture a title.

V. Evaluation

Complete the "Alabama Check-Up" worksheet.

ALABAMA

Draw pictures or use sentences, jingles, cartoons, or other creative means to show interesting facts, thoughts, or ideas about Alabama. Try to show as many things as possible that you have learned. (The last three boxes are for your own topics.)

State Flag	State Flower	State Bird
Minerals	Crops	Recreation
Industries	Neighboring States	Natural Resources

ARKANSAS

The Land Of Opportunity

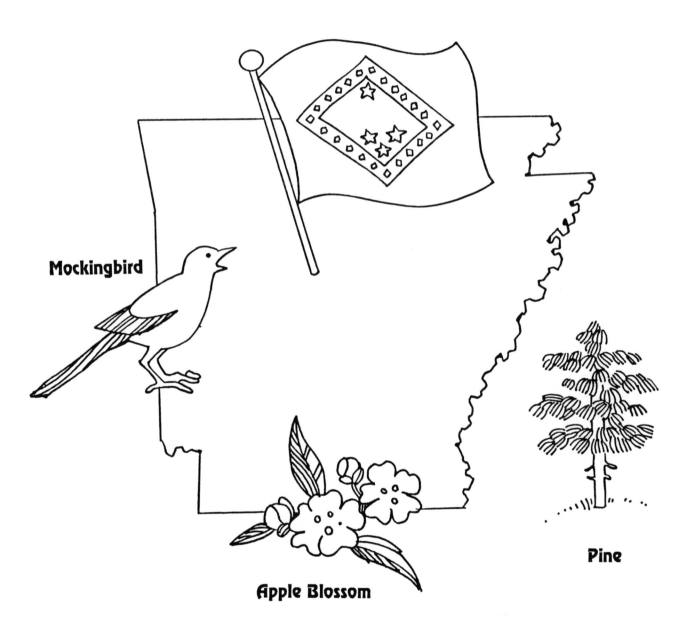

Mockingbird

Apple Blossom

Pine

ARKANSAS

Fact • Sheet

─────────────────── **FAST FACTS** ───────

1. **CAPITAL:** Little Rock

2. **BORDERING STATES:** Louisiana, Texas, Oklahoma, Missouri, Tennessee, Mississippi

3. **THREE MAJOR CITIES:** Little Rock • Fort Smith • North Little Rock

4. **ADMITTED TO UNION:** June 15, 1836

OTHER INTERESTING FACTS:

1. ❑ A unique and almost unbelievable feature of Arkansas is the Crater of Diamonds State Park. This 78-acre field is North America's only public diamond field. It attracts hordes of visitors, who are given the opportunity to dig for diamonds—and the rule is finders keepers!

2. ❑ All of Arkansas's rivers, with the exception of the Buffalo River, have been dammed. By a 1972 Act of Congress, the Buffalo was designated a National River in order to preserve its natural beauty and to protect the plant and animal life native to its banks.

3. ❑ Arkansas's fertile farmland yields cotton, soybeans, and watermelons. Rice is also an important crop. As a matter of fact, people are often surprised to learn that more rice is grown in Arkansas than in any other state in the Union. This rice supply is important to the wild geese and ducks who stop in Arkansas to feed during their migrations to and from the warm climate of the Gulf of Mexico.

SUPER FACT: *Did you know* that Texarkana is a town that straddles the border of Arkansas and Texas? If you lived in Texarkana, you might brush your teeth in Arkansas, buy your groceries in Texas, go to the dentist in Arkansas, and have lunch in Texas, all in half a day—just by crossing and recrossing the state line.

ARKANSAS

Unit•At•A•Glance

Read and complete all activities, beginning with **I** and ending with **V.**

I. Language

Write a letter to a new Arkansas pen pal. Share some of the highlights of your own state with the pen pal and ask questions about Arkansas. Try to word your questions to help you gain ideas and information about Arkansas's history as well as present-day high points.

II. Environmental Studies

In each list below, one word does not belong. Mark out the word that does not pertain to Arkansas and tell why it is a misfit. Tell how the other words relate to each other and to the state.

cotton	Dallas	recreation
soybeans	Little Rock	farming
rice	Fort Smith	mining
pineapples	Texarkana	shrimping

III. Math

Make up four fraction problems about the weight and size of Arkansas-grown watermelons. Ask a friend to solve your problems. Check the answers.

IV. Enrichment

Use the following words and add five of your own to make a picture dictionary to help a younger child learn about Arkansas:
- watermelons
- mallard ducks
- diamonds
- mockingbird
- rice
- apple blossom

V. Evaluation

Complete the "Arkansas Check-Up" worksheet.

© 1993 by Incentive Publications, Inc., Nashville, TN.

65

ARKANSAS

Check•Up

Use pictures, words, phrases, sentences, symbols, or poems to complete the Arkansas Wheel of Fame to show what you know about the "Land of Opportunity State."

FLORIDA

The Sunshine State

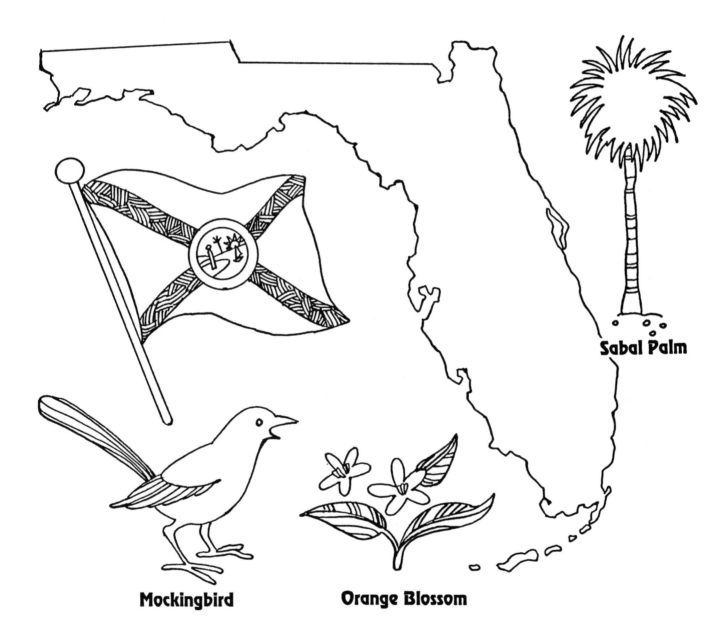

Sabal Palm

Mockingbird

Orange Blossom

FLORIDA

Fact • Sheet

-------- FAST FACTS --------

1. **CAPITAL:** Tallahassee

2. **BORDERING STATES:** Alabama, Georgia

3. **THREE MAJOR CITIES:** Jacksonville • Miami • Tampa

4. **ADMITTED TO UNION:** March 3, 1845

OTHER INTERESTING FACTS:

1. Florida's plant and animal wildlife is as interesting and as diverse as that of any state in the Union. From alligators to pelicans, sea cows to sea horses, palm groves to sea grass, sponges to coral, and snails to wildcats, Florida's natural treasures continue to fascinate nature lovers of all ages. Many of these plants and animals have been placed on the endangered species list and are now protected by very strict regulations.

2. Tourism and retirement residents are important to Florida's economy. Vacationers from all areas of the world come to enjoy the beaches, Disney World, and the multitude of rivers and lakes. There are no mountains in Florida.

3. Florida's citrus industry is located in its central region where most of Florida's hills are to be found. Citrus farming is both hard work and a chancy occupation. A hard freeze can wipe out an entire crop. Growers have to watch the weather and move quickly to bring a crop to harvest.

SUPER FACT: *Did you know* Florida produces a quarter of the world's oranges and other citrus fruit?

Unit•At•A•Glance

Read and complete all activities, beginning with **I** and ending with **V.**

I. Language

Stories and legends of pirates and pirate ships of old that found shelter in Florida's harbors and channels are part of the state's rich heritage. Write a pirate story of your own—making sure to tell who, where, what, and when—and give your story a happy ending.

II. Environmental Studies

Select one plant or animal native to Florida that is currently on the endangered species list. Research the history and habitat of this species. Describe its unique features. Identify sources of danger to this species. Design a poster with a slogan to help protect this plant or animal.

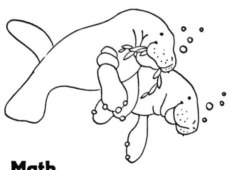

III. Math

Make up four math word problems that have to do with citrus farming. Make one division, one addition, one subtraction, and one multiplication problem. Ask a friend to solve your problems. Check the answers.

IV. Enrichment

Design (on paper) an original piece of jewelry or a household item to be made from shells, beach glass, driftwood, pebbles, and/or other treasures to be found on Florida's beaches. List the items used and tell where each would be found.

V. Evaluation

Complete the "Florida Check-Up" worksheet.

FLORIDA

Check•Up

Complete your own Florida Facts, Thoughts, and Opinions Wheel by drawing pictures and writing words, phrases, jingles, paragraphs, poems, cartoons, or other creative expressions between each spoke of the wheel. Try to show as many things as possible that you have learned about Florida.

GEORGIA

The Peach State

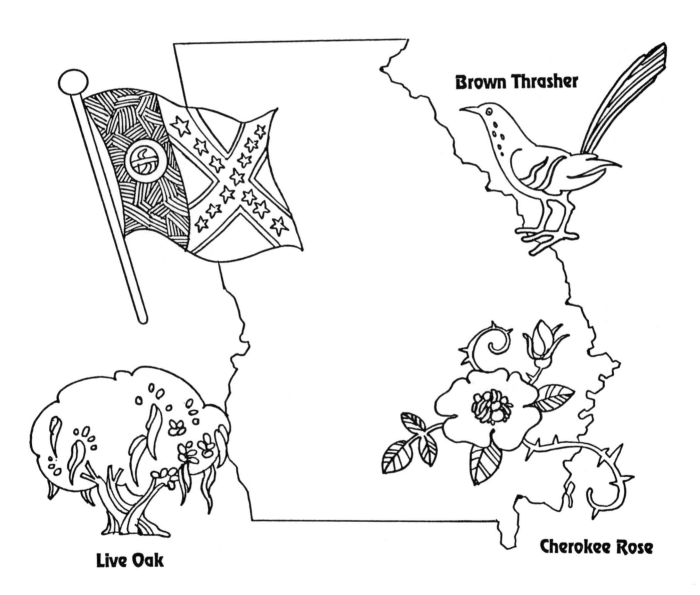

Brown Thrasher

Live Oak

Cherokee Rose

GEORGIA

Fact • Sheet

1. **CAPITAL:** Atlanta

2. **BORDERING STATES:** Alabama, Tennessee, North Carolina, South Carolina, Florida

3. **THREE MAJOR CITIES:** Atlanta • Columbus • Savannah

4. **ADMITTED TO UNION:** January 2, 1788

OTHER INTERESTING FACTS:

1. Georgia is the largest state east of the Mississippi. Swamps, mountains, sea coast, flatlands, and hills are all found in Georgia. Stone Mountain, Georgia, is the world's largest isolated block of raw granite.

2. Agriculture is important to Georgia's economy. Soybeans, cotton, vegetables, fruits, nuts, and tobacco, as well as hogs, poultry, and cattle are grown here, but the two best-known agricultural products are peanuts and peaches. Georgia grows and ships more peanuts than any other state. Peanut butter, peanut oil, and other peanut products are processed in Georgia, providing many jobs for the state's residents.

3. The FOXFIRE books, which chronicle mountain life and offer advice and information to people who want to live the simple life, are published in Rabun, Georgia.

SUPER FACT: *Did you know* that the statue of Lincoln in the Lincoln Memorial in Washington, D.C., is made of Georgia marble?

Unit•At•A•Glance

Read and complete all activities, beginning with **I** and ending with **V**.

I. Language

Select the one place in Georgia that you would most like to visit. Write a travel guide for yourself. List methods of transportation, traveling companions, major points of interest, clothes needed, recreation or entertainment, and length of visit.

II. Environmental Studies

Design simple symbols for the physical feature listed below and use them to locate the features on an outline map of Georgia.

- islands
- citrus groves
- mountains
- wildlife reserve
- cities
- coastline
- farmland
- cattle area

III. Math

Ask each of five friends to select from this list their favorite way to eat peaches:

- peach pie
- peach ice cream
- whole ripe peach
- peach yogurt
- sliced peaches with cream

Graph the results and share your findings with the people you interviewed. You might also tell them that Georgia is the third largest peach-growing state.

IV. Enrichment

Draw and cut out two peanut finger puppets with personalities of their own. Write a puppet play using puns, knock-knock jokes, or other funny sayings. Remind everyone who sees your play that Georgia is the peanut capital of the United States.

V. Evaluation

Complete the "Georgia Check-Up" worksheet.

GEORGIA

Check•Up

Finish the following four sentences in four minutes or less:

1. The state flower of Georgia is _____.

2. The state bird of Georgia is _____.

3. The capital of Georgia is _____.

4. Two other major cities of Georgia are _____ and _____.

On the back of this page, write just one sentence to tell the first thing you would do if . . .

1. You inherited a peanut butter factory in Georgia.

2. You were invited to be editor of the next edition of the FOXFIRE books.

3. You won an all-expenses-paid trip to visit Stone Mountain, Georgia.

4. You woke up one morning to find yourself on the top floor of an Atlanta high rise hotel.

5. You were designated to develop an *official* nickname for Georgia (it does not have one).

6. You and your family were planning a vacation trip to one of Georgia's Sea Islands.

KENTUCKY

The Bluegrass State

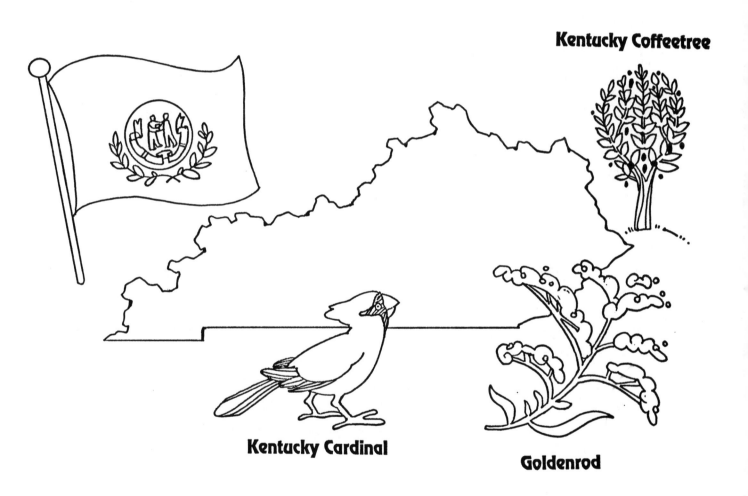

Kentucky Coffeetree

Kentucky Cardinal

Goldenrod

KENTUCKY

Fact • Sheet

FAST FACTS

1. **CAPITAL:** Frankfort

2. **BORDERING STATES:** Missouri, Illinois, Indiana, Ohio, West Virginia, Virginia, Tennessee

3. **THREE MAJOR CITIES:** Louisville • Lexington • Owensboro

4. **ADMITTED TO UNION:** June 1, 1792

OTHER INTERESTING FACTS:

1. What is Black Gold? It is the valuable dark coal that has long been an important source of income for the state of Kentucky. Kentucky coal was formed more than 300 million years ago when plants from the swamp died, decayed, and then were pressed, heated, and hardened into black coal by deposits of mud and sand. Burning coal does cause air pollution, but a nation that desperately needs energy has continued to use coal for fuel. Coal is not Kentucky's only natural resource—it also has stone, natural gas, sand, and gravel.

2. Breeders, trainers, riders, grooms, investors, veterinarians, and auctioneers are just some of the people who work in occupations associated with the thoroughbred industry. Thoroughbred horse farms are seen all over the Bluegrass region of Kentucky. These farms have contributed much to the economy, history, and culture of the state.

3. The Mammoth Cave National Park system, with more than 300 miles of mapped passageways, is the largest underground cave system in the world. The caves were formed as rainwater sank into the ground and slowly destroyed the limestone beneath the surface

SUPER FACT: *Did you know* that the world's largest gold depository is at the Fort Knox, Kentucky, military reservation?

Unit•At•A•Glance

Read and complete all activities, beginning with **I** and ending with **V**.

I. Language

What do people mean when they say "I am as hungry as a horse?" Write two new similes, each comparing something to a thoroughbred horse.

II. Environmental Studies

List the advantages and disadvantages of mining and using soft coal for energy. Write a paragraph stating and supporting your opinions.

III. Math

List three ways each of the following would use math every day:
- veterinarian
- miner
- farmer

Name the math skills each would need.

IV. Enrichment

Design a new flag and a logo for Kentucky. Use a picture or symbol of one of the resources you have learned about as the focus of your design.

V. Evaluation

Complete the "Kentucky Check-Up" worksheet.

KENTUCKY

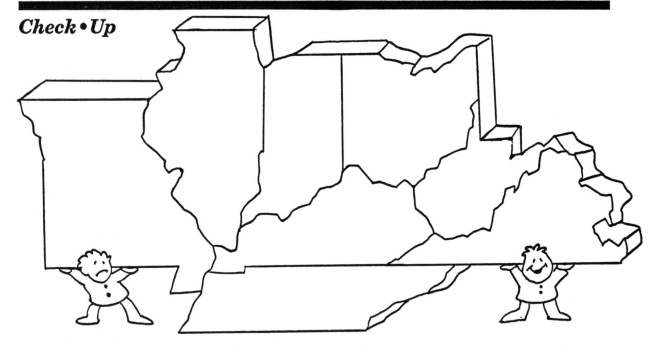

1. Indicate the capital of Kentucky with a dot inside the state outline and write the capital's name next to the dot.

2. Write the name of each of the seven states that border Kentucky inside the correct state outline.

3. Draw and color a picture of the Kentucky state bird and state flower.

4. List three important facts about the state of Kentucky.

_____

_____

_____

LOUISIANA

The Pelican State

Brown Pelican

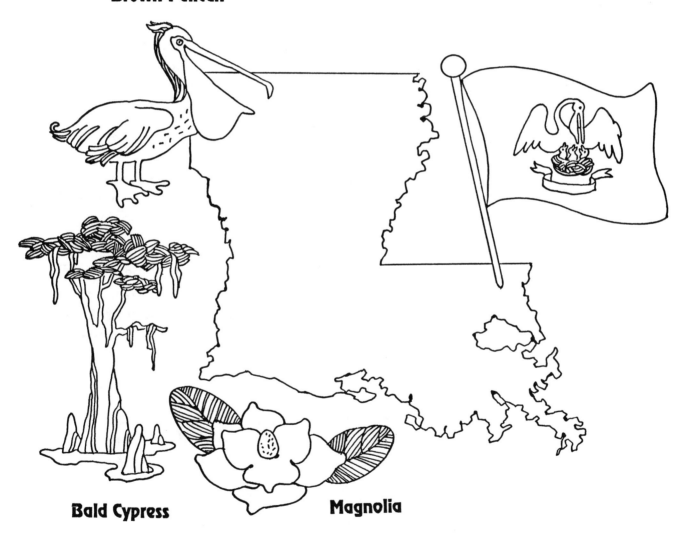

Bald Cypress

Magnolia

LOUISIANA

Fact • Sheet

───────────────────────────────── FAST FACTS ──

1. **CAPITAL:** Baton Rouge

2. **BORDERING STATES:** Texas, Arkansas, Mississippi

3. **THREE MAJOR CITIES:** New Orleans • Baton Rouge • Shreveport

4. **ADMITTED TO UNION:** April 30, 1812

OTHER INTERESTING FACTS:

1. People of many heritages joined the French and Spanish colonists to make up a colorful and diverse population, which makes Louisiana one of the nation's most exciting states. The Mardi Gras celebration in New Orleans is a good time to experience the music, dancing, folklore, and delectable foods for which the state is famous, and to get a taste of the diverse cultures and Old World customs still present in Louisiana.

2. In addition to music and fun, industries flourish in Louisiana. The Mississippi River provides an abundant water supply and a means of transportation for manufacturers. Some of the crops grown for export to other countries as well as to other states are cotton, sugar cane, soybeans, and rice.

3. The Mississippi River has been walled with levees or concrete walls in order to change its course, straightening it in places. Many towns that were once right on the river are no longer river cities—they are now known as "high and dry" towns. The people have also built floodways in order to drain floodwater into the Gulf of Mexico.

SUPER FACT: *Did you know* that Louisiana crawfish are used in both country Cajun and city Creole cooking, and are regarded throughout the state as a fine delicacy worthy of recognizing with festivals and parades?

LOUISIANA

Unit•At•A•Glance

Read and complete all activities, beginning with **I** and ending with **V**.

I. Language

Develop an outline for the study of Louisiana. List the big ideas that you want to learn about and order each big idea. Then, under each big idea, make a list of the more specific things you want to find out. List information resources to be used and logical steps to follow to complete the study. Order the steps and the method you will use to organize, evaluate, and present your findings.

II. Environmental Studies

List six to twelve things that would be grown inside the boundaries of Louisiana and distributed beyond those boundaries.

III. Math

Pretend that you have a budget of $125 per person per day for five days for you and a friend to visit New Orleans during Mardi Gras. The hotel where you will stay will cost you $45.00 a day per person, tickets for the Mardi Gras party you want to attend each day are $37.00 per couple, three meals a day will cost $27.00 per person per day, and public transportation to the parade and events on your schedule will be $16.00 per person per day. Add these expenses and subtract the total from the budgeted amount to find out how much you will have left for souvenirs and miscellaneous expenses.

IV. Enrichment

Design a Mardi Gras costume, complete with mask, shoes, and a banner, to be carried in the parade. Specify the colors, materials, and directions for making the costume and banner.

V. Evaluation

Complete the "Louisiana Check-Up" worksheet.

LOUISIANA

Check•Up

Make up twelve questions with answers for a Louisiana Trivia game. Check your Fact Sheet and other references to be sure your answers are correct. Write your questions and answers here. Later, ask a friend to make up twelve questions and answers. Combine your questions and answers and play Louisiana Trivia.

Questions   Answers

1. _____   1. _____
   _____   _____

2. _____   2. _____
   _____   _____

3. _____   3. _____
   _____   _____

4. _____   4. _____
   _____   _____

5. _____   5. _____
   _____   _____

6. _____   6. _____
   _____   _____

7. _____   7. _____
   _____   _____

8. _____   8. _____
   _____   _____

9. _____   9. _____
   _____   _____

10. _____   10. _____
    _____   _____

11. _____   11. _____
    _____   _____

12. _____   12. _____
    _____   _____

MISSISSIPPI

The Magnolia State

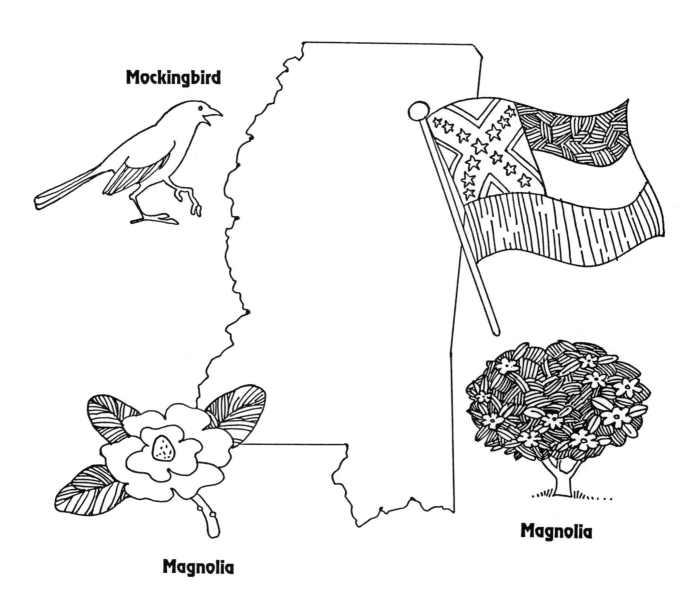

Mockingbird

Magnolia

Magnolia

MISSISSIPPI

Fact • Sheet

```
┌─────────────────────────────── FAST FACTS ───┐
│                                                │
│  1. CAPITAL: Jackson                           │
│                                                │
│  2. BORDERING STATES: Alabama, Tennessee,      │
│     Louisiana, Arkansas                        │
│                                                │
│  3. THREE MAJOR CITIES: Jackson • Biloxi •     │
│     Greenville                                 │
│                                                │
│  4. ADMITTED TO UNION: December 10, 1817       │
│                                                │
└────────────────────────────────────────────────┘
```

OTHER INTERESTING FACTS:

1. The Mississippi River has played a mighty role in Mississippi's history, especially in the history of its commerce. Towns sprang up because of "river traffic." Just as quickly, towns were deserted when the river's course changed, causing floods, or leaving towns high and dry. When railroads and highways appeared, taking away much of the river's transportation importance, many more river towns disappeared. In recent years, the Mississippi has become important again, as river barges carry sand, gravel, coal, and grain along the river. Tourists also travel the river for pleasure, disembarking from pleasure boats to visit plantations and museums and to see other sights.

2. Fishing has always been of great commercial importance to Mississippi. The Mississippi River is fished for fresh-water fish, while fishermen on vessels on the Gulf Coast fish for shrimp, oysters, and other shellfish. Those vacationers who go to the Gulf Coast for more than sun and sand may fish for pleasure. Fish are also "grown" in ponds on catfish farms!

3. Mississippi has been known as an agricultural state, but many people are moving to its industrialized communities where jobs are more plentiful. The state government began a program to "Balance Agriculture With Industry," until finally, in the mid-1960's, there were more Mississippians with jobs in industry than in agriculture.

SUPER FACT: *Did you know* that the University of Mississippi houses the oldest book in America? It is an ancient Biblical manuscript.

Unit•At•A•Glance

Read and complete all activities, beginning with **I** and ending with **V**.

I. Language

Make a list of ten questions about the state of Mississippi. Ask people you know to supply answers for your questions. Write down their answers. Use your Fact Sheet and additional references to check their answers.

II. Environmental Studies

Write a story about a day in the life of a Mississippi catfish farmer. Draw and color pictures to illustrate your story.

III. Math

Use the questions from the language activity to develop ten word problems for a friend to solve. Ask the friend to use the answer to develop ten problems for you to solve. Check each other's work and have fun matching answers and questions.

IV. Enrichment

Plan one full day's schedule (from breakfast to bedtime) for passengers aboard a paddle wheel boat traveling up the Mississippi River. List menus (including three meals and snacks), daytime activities, and an evening show, complete with band and entertainers. Make it an exciting day!

V. Evaluation

Complete the "Mississippi Check-Up" worksheet.

MISSISSIPPI

Check•Up

Think of words, phrases, symbols, or pictures to show what you have learned about Mississippi. Each should begin with a different letter of the alphabet. Draw and/or write as many of them as you can in the space below.

NORTH CAROLINA

The Tar Heel State

Pine

Flowering Dogwood

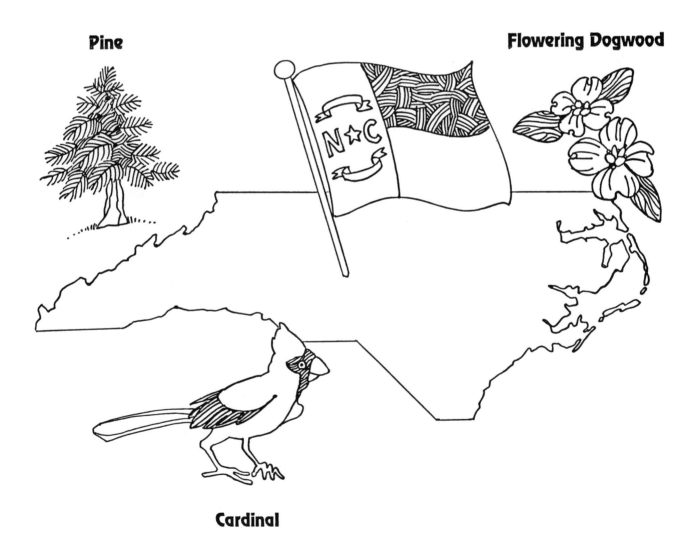

Cardinal

NORTH CAROLINA

Fact • Sheet

── FAST FACTS ──

1. **CAPITAL:** Raleigh

2. **BORDERING STATES:** South Carolina, Georgia, Tennessee, Virginia

3. **THREE MAJOR CITIES:** Charlotte • Raleigh • Greensboro

4. **ADMITTED TO UNION:** November 21, 1789

OTHER INTERESTING FACTS:

1. From North Carolina's large mountain range to its long coastline, this state is known for its natural beauty and abundant plant and animal wildlife. It is a wide state, encompassing many differing land formations and affording a variety of occupations and lifestyles.

2. North Carolina's famous barrier islands of the outer banks are constantly being shaped and reshaped by the shifting sands caused by pounding waves and heavy storms. Radar now replaces many of the lighthouses that formerly dotted these islands. Actually it is these islands that protect the mainland from being battered by the mighty Atlantic Ocean.

3. Farming and timbering are important industries, but North Carolina is also well supplied with textile and furniture manufacturing plants, and with medical, industrial, and business management research institutions.

SUPER FACT: *Did you know* that North Carolina manufactures more tobacco products than do all the other states put together?

Unit•At•A•Glance

Read and complete all activities, beginning with **I** and ending with **V.**

I. Language

Write the script (introduction, questions and answers, and "wrap-up") for a TV program based on the state of North Carolina. Name a company/sponsor for the program and write two commercials to be used during the program.

II. Environmental Studies

Compare and contrast the natural resources, physical features, crops, and industries of North Carolina with those of your state.

III. Math

Tell how each of the following persons would use math skills in connection with his or her everyday job. List the skills he or she would need.
- tobacco auctioneer
- lighthouse keeper
- research scientist
- textile mill personnel manager

IV. Enrichment

Paste or glue scraps of paper (construction, tissue, drawing, gift wrap, or whatever you have) to a sheet of drawing paper to make a torn-paper collage showing a North Carolina sunrise or sunset over the mountains, fields, or shoreline. Show as many details as possible and try to give your work your best "artistic flair." Just remember, it's a *torn-paper* collage; that means no scissors allowed!

V. Evaluation

Complete the "North Carolina Check-Up" worksheet.

NORTH CAROLINA

Check • Up

Imagine that people from each state in the Union are to design and make a patchwork quilt to represent their state in a museum exhibit to be shown in Washington, D.C. You have been asked to design the quilt to be made for North Carolina. Use words, phrases, pictures, and symbols to tell as much as possible about North Carolina.

SOUTH CAROLINA

The Palmetto State

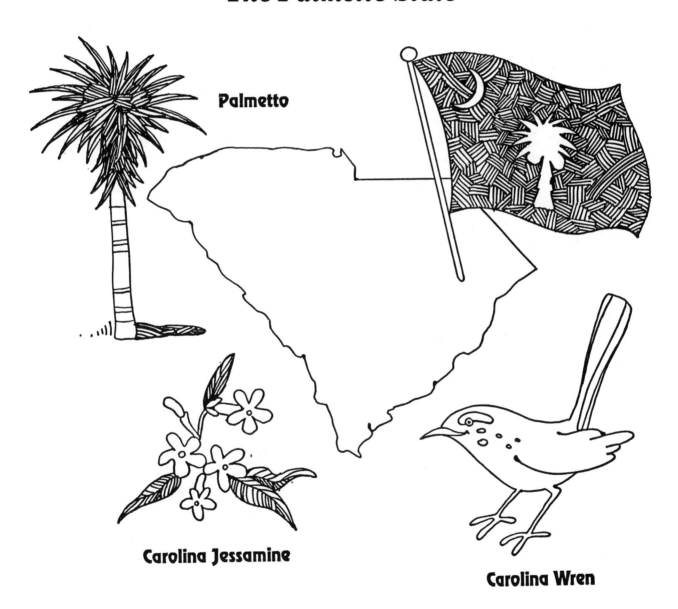

Palmetto

Carolina Jessamine

Carolina Wren

SOUTH CAROLINA

Fact • Sheet

FAST FACTS

1. **CAPITAL:** Columbia

2. **BORDERING STATES:** North Carolina, Georgia

3. **THREE MAJOR CITIES:** Columbia • Charleston • North Charleston

4. **ADMITTED TO UNION:** May 23, 1788

OTHER INTERESTING FACTS:

1. Cotton used to be essential to South Carolina's economy because it brought in more cash than any other crop. Now it is important to the economy in a different way—cotton is brought into the state to be used as raw material for South Carolina's textile mills. This state is a prime location for these mills because of the availability of labor and because of the electricity that is generated by hydroelectric power plants on the state's many rivers. Foreign companies as well as companies from all over the United States have located factories in South Carolina for these reasons.

2. What have South Carolinians planted in the worn-out soil that cotton left behind? Peach trees, for one thing—now only California produces more peaches than South Carolina. There are also fast-growing loblolly pines, which are large enough to be cut 15 to 20 years after planting, and grass, planted to feed the beef cattle now raised in the state.

3. Charleston is one of the country's loveliest old cities. It is a harbor city, rich in history and folklore. The people of Charleston have worked hard to preserve the flavor of the "Old South." At the same time, they have developed a progressive city that provides good jobs and modern conveniences for its citizens. Many people visit Charleston to tour the beautiful old homes and museums to learn more about our country's history.

SUPER FACT: *Did you know* that South Carolina was the first state to secede from the Union at the beginning of the War Between the States?

SOUTH CAROLINA

Unit•At•A•Glance

Read and complete all activities, beginning with **I** and ending with **V**.

I. Language

Create a crossword or word-find puzzle using the following ten words, plus ten others selected to represent the facts related to your study of South Carolina.

(1) textiles   (6) mills
(2) cotton   (7) plantations
(3) electricity   (8) oysters
(4) machinery   (9) rice
(5) hills   (10) South

II. Environmental Studies

List five qualities that the supervisor of a large textile mill today should have. How do these compare with the qualities that are desirable in the manager of a large farm?

III. Math

Create a timeline for the history of South Carolina. Begin with the date it was admitted to the Union (May 23, 1788) and end with this year.

IV. Enrichment

South Carolina is well known for its fine foods. Okra, rice, yams, ham, oysters, and peaches are some of the most popular ingredients used in festive recipes. Make up a menu for a special celebration. Create an original recipe using one of these foods.

V. Evaluation

Complete the "South Carolina Check-Up" worksheet.

SOUTH CAROLINA

Check•Up

Pretend that you have been asked to write a full-page encyclopedia entry about South Carolina. Begin with the bare facts and end with as much interesting information as you can. Just remember, the facts and information must be 100% accurate.

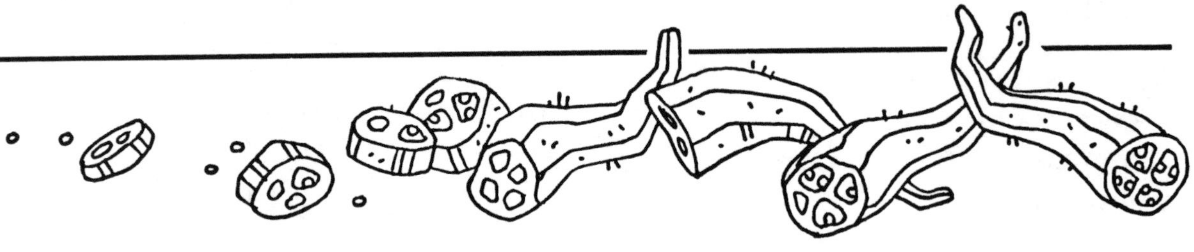

_____

_____

_____

_____

_____

_____

_____

_____

_____

_____

_____

_____

_____

_____

_____

_____

_____

_____

TENNESSEE

The Volunteer State

Tulip Poplar

Iris

Mockingbird

TENNESSEE

Fact • Sheet

1. **CAPITAL:** Nashville

2. **BORDERING STATES:** Kentucky, Virginia, North Carolina, Georgia, Alabama, Mississippi, Arkansas, Missouri

3. **THREE MAJOR CITIES:** Memphis • Nashville • Knoxville

4. **ADMITTED TO UNION:** June 1, 1796

OTHER INTERESTING FACTS:

1. ❑ The people of Tennessee historically have been valorous in battle. The nickname "The Volunteer State" originated during the War of 1812, when volunteer soldiers from Tennessee, serving under Andrew Jackson, showed great courage during the Battle of New Orleans. One famous early settler of Tennessee was Davy Crockett. He was a frontier hunter and west Tennessee congressman who later moved to Texas. In 1836 he died in the Battle of the Alamo during the Texas fight for independence.

2. ❑ Tennessee is known for its music the world over. Memphis, in West Tennessee, is known as the "home of the blues." Nashville, in the central part of the state, is celebrated for its country music and the Grand Ole Opry. In many parts of East Tennessee, folk music is enjoyed in the same form as it was a hundred years ago.

3. ❑ A large portion of the Great Smoky Mountains National Park lies in East Tennessee. Many visitors enjoy its beautiful campsites and trails, appealing wildlife, lovely streams, and mountain crafts and folkways. The highest point in Tennessee is Clingman's Dome. At 6,643 feet, Clingman's Dome is also the highest peak in the Great Smoky Mountains and the highest point along the famous Appalachian Trail.

SUPER FACT: *Did you know* that the town of Shelbyville, Tennessee, is known as the "Pencil Capital of the World" because of the large number of pencils that are manufactured there? It is also known as the "Tennessee Walking Horse Capital of the World." The famous Tennessee Walking Horse is raised, trained, and shown in this small town.

Unit•At•A•Glance

Read and complete all activities, beginning with **I** and ending with **V**.

I. Language

Write a creative story about a courageous act performed by a boy or girl living in Tennessee in pioneer days. Be sure to include who, when, where, what, and how.

II. Environmental Studies

Tennessee is bordered by eight states. List these states in alphabetical order. Beside each state write the name of its capital and its largest city.

III. Math

Make up five math word problems about Tennessee and Tennesseans. Exchange problems with a friend and solve the problems.

IV. Enrichment

Even though agriculture is not as important to Tennessee as it once was, many Tennesseans still make their living by farming. Draw and color a picture to show a modern Tennessee farm scene. Add as much detail as you can.

V. Evaluation

Complete the "Tennessee Check-Up" worksheet.

TENNESSEE

Check•Up

Find the words in the puzzle to fill in the blanks in the sentences below. You will find the words across, up, and down.

M	O	C	K	I	N	G	B	I	R	D	K	A	D
C	D	R	O	R	N	K	S	T	R	O	N	V	O
U	M	S	C	A	B	C	D	E	E	G	O	O	P
M	E	M	P	H	I	S	Y	H	I	J	X	L	A
B	L	U	E	S	R	K	R	L	M	N	V	U	L
E	O	P	R	Y	I	S	P	T	U	V	I	N	Q
R	I	V	E	R	S	M	O	K	Y	E	L	T	R
L	S	O	U	T	H	E	R	N	W	X	L	E	S
A	Y	Z	A	B	C	D	E	F	G	H	E	E	B
N	A	S	H	V	I	L	L	E	I	J	K	R	U
D	A	V	Y	C	R	O	C	K	E	T	T	S	M

1. The _____ is the Tennessee state flower.

2. The Great _____ Mountains National Park is located in Tennessee.

3. A famous Tennessee frontier hunter was named _____

   _____.

4. _____ is the capital of Tennessee.

5. Tennessee's nickname is the _____ State.

6. The two major cities in Tennessee, other than the capital, are

   _____ and _____.

7. Memphis is known as the home of the _____ and Nashville

   is known as the home of the Grand Ole _____.

8. Tennessee is a _____, not a northern, state.

VIRGINIA

Old Dominion

Flowering Dogwood

Cardinal

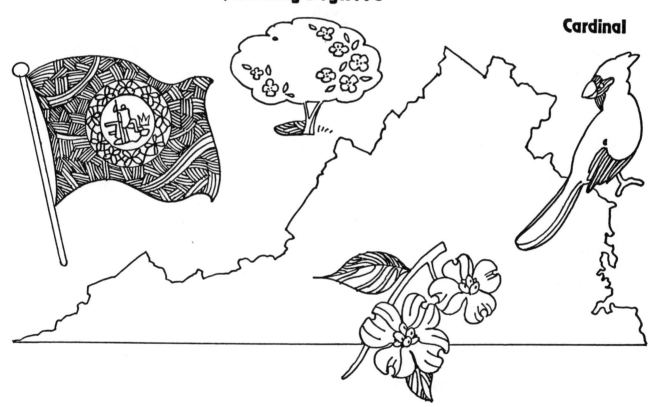

Flowering Dogwood

VIRGINIA

Fact • Sheet

FAST FACTS

1. **CAPITAL:** Richmond

2. **BORDERING STATES:** Maryland, West Virginia, Kentucky, Tennessee, North Carolina

3. **THREE MAJOR CITIES:** Virginia Beach • Norfolk • Richmond

4. **ADMITTED TO UNION:** June 25, 1788

OTHER INTERESTING FACTS:

1. People who live in Alexandria, Virginia, drive along the very streets in which George Washington drilled his troops. People who live in Roanoke live near the place where Booker T. Washington was born a slave. People in Richmond who attend St. John's Church attend the church in which Patrick Henry said his famous words: "Give me liberty or give me death!" Traces of history are all around this state.

2. Virginia was attractive to early colonists, with its good harbors, a gentle climate, and rich soil. Early settlers planted tobacco and sold it to English buyers. Tobacco, along with coal, is still exported from four coastal cities: Hampton, Newport News, Portsmouth, and Chesapeake. The largest naval base in the country is in Norfolk, and bustling shipyards are located in Newport News.

3. The first rayon factory was opened in Roanoke in 1917. One step in the rayon-making process is the grinding of loblolly pine into pulp (some of the pulp is also made into paper). Virginia growers grow loblolly pine, peanuts, and soybeans. On the Delmarva Peninsula, across Chesapeake Bay, farmers grow food to sell to city people.

SUPER FACT: *Did you know* that the crop John Rolfe began growing in Virginia in 1612 still provides more income than does any other crop in the state? It is tobacco.

VIRGINIA

Read and complete all activities, beginning with **I** and ending with **V**.

I. Language

Select one of the following topics to use as the basis for a creative story with a modern-day Virginia setting:
- Working in a Newport News shipyard is not always easy.
- Give me liberty or give me death!
- Growing up on a Virginia tobacco farm
- Virginia, the state of heroes, gives us another one.

II. Environmental Studies

Write a definitive sentence stating the greatest contribution to the nation made by each of the following persons:
- George Washington
- Patrick Henry
- Booker T. Washington

Place in rank order (in your opinion) these contributions in terms of their importance to the growth of democracy in the United States.

III. Math

Survey four people to find out which of these statements they believe. (They may believe all of them)
- Virginia is one of the most important states in the Union.
- Virginia would be a great place to live and work.
- Most of the people now living in Virginia are three-generation residents.

Graph your findings.

IV. Enrichment

Draw, color, and cut out pictures of three persons participating in different river-related sports in Virginia. Arrange and paste the pictures on drawing paper to make a collage. Color in a background and give your collage a title.

V. Evaluation

Complete the "Virginia Check-Up" worksheet.

VIRGINIA

Check•Up

Make a list of twenty spelling words for a Virginia Spelling Bee. Use words related to the state's history, heroes, geography, culture, symbols, occupations, recreation, natural resources, and other important features. Be sure you can spell all the words, then write a definition beside each. Test a friend's spelling skills and knowledge of Virginia.

1. _____ _____
2. _____ _____
3. _____ _____
4. _____ _____
5. _____ _____
6. _____ _____
7. _____ _____
8. _____ _____
9. _____ _____
10. _____ _____
11. _____ _____
12. _____ _____
13. _____ _____
14. _____ _____
15. _____ _____
16. _____ _____
17. _____ _____
18. _____ _____
19. _____ _____
20. _____ _____

WEST VIRGINIA

The Mountain State

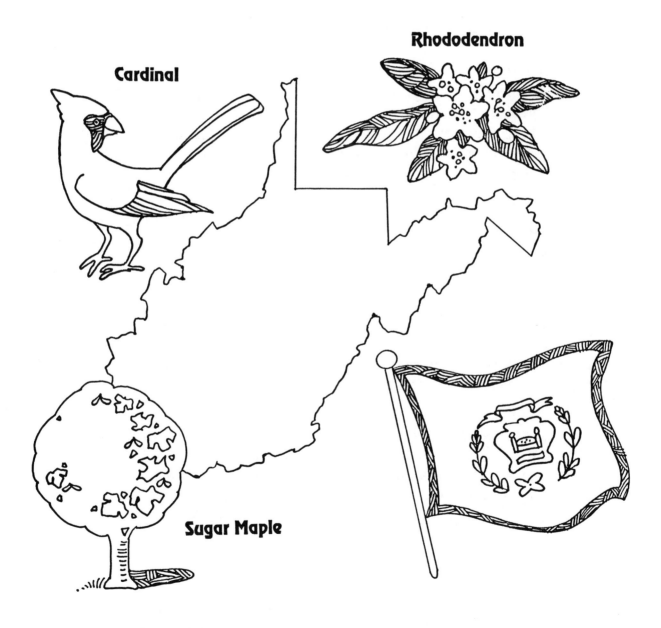

Cardinal

Rhododendron

Sugar Maple

WEST VIRGINIA

Fact • Sheet

─────────────── **FAST FACTS** ───────────────

1. **CAPITAL:** Charleston

2. **BORDERING STATES:** Virginia, Kentucky, Ohio, Pennsylvania, Maryland

3. **THREE MAJOR CITIES:** Charleston • Huntington • Wheeling

4. **ADMITTED TO UNION:** June 20, 1863

OTHER INTERESTING FACTS:

1. It's difficult to find a piece of flat land in West Virginia, except for land in the river valleys. There are many songs about the hills of West Virginia. Indeed, the state motto is Montani Semper Liberi, which means, "Mountaineers Are Always Free." The numerous mountains and rushing rivers combine to produce lots of wild water called "white water." The oldest river in North America is called, oddly enough, the New River, and is located in West Virginia. It is famous for its rapids. It is an exhilarating sport to canoe or kayak in these sometimes-dangerous waters, and many canoe and kayak meets are held in the state. The canoes are made of modern materials, but they retain the birch-bark canoe design of the Native Americans.

2. West Virginia has long been known as a coal miner's state, with its abundant bituminous, or soft coal beds. Most West Virginia coal miners, however, have been replaced by machinery. Today, more West Virginians work in industry than in the coal mines.

3. Glass and pottery industries have been important in West Virginia since its early history. Pottery was made by Native Americans, and some pottery today is made the same way it has been for hundred of years. The state is rich in clay that is good for pottery-making, as well as in the silica sand and limestone that is necessary for glass production.

SUPER FACT: *Did you know* that most of the marbles made in the United States were made in West Virginia? If you play a game of marbles, chances are that the marbles you are playing with came from West Virginia.

Unit•At•A•Glance

Read and complete all activities, beginning with **I** and ending with **V.**

I. Language

Many of America's treasured tall tales have come from the West Virginia mountains. Make up a tall tale with a West Virginia setting. Be creative. Make your tall tale as exciting as you can.

II. Environmental Studies

Think of what you have learned about West Virginia. Make a list of ten possible occupations that young people entering the job market in West Virginia today might be trained for.

III. Math

Make up three math problems related to the roaring rivers of West Virginia. Write each problem on a separate index card or strip of paper. Ask three friends to solve your problems, then exchange and check each other's answers. You will check all three, of course.

IV. Enrichment

Paste or tape paper strips together to make a long, narrow banner. Rewrite your West Virginia tall tale on the strip. Use creative lettering, signs, symbols, and illustrations to add interest. Roll, wrap, and paste the top of the strip around a pencil, add a string for hanging, and display your tall tale for others to enjoy.

V. Evaluation

Complete the "West Virginia Check-Up" worksheet.

WEST VIRGINIA

Check•Up

Create a display for your school library to show what you have learned about West Virginia. Remember to include geography, natural resources, occupations, legend and lore, state symbols, and other interesting information. Sketch the setup and items for your display below. Label all the items.

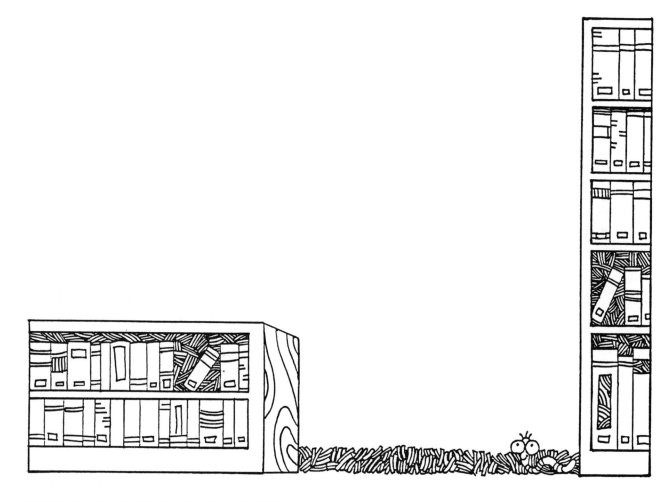

Great Lakes States

ILLINOIS

The Land of Lincoln

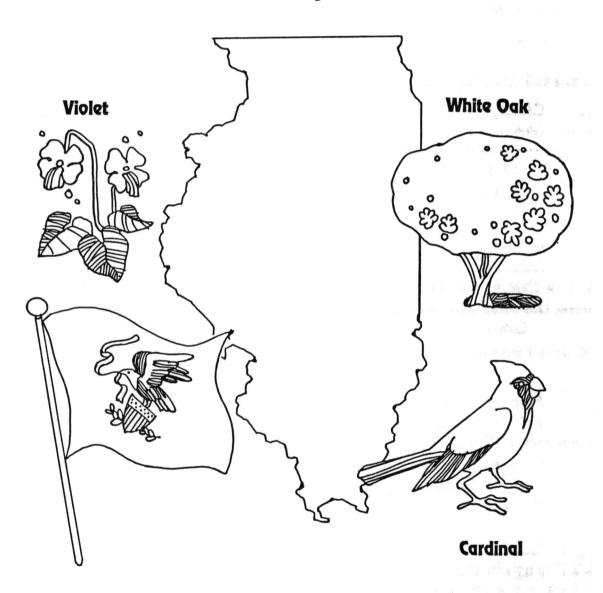

Violet

White Oak

Cardinal

ILLINOIS

Fact • Sheet

1. **CAPITAL:** Springfield

2. **BORDERING STATES:** Missouri, Iowa, Wisconsin, Indiana, Kentucky

3. **THREE MAJOR CITIES:** Chicago • Rockford • Peoria

4. **ADMITTED TO UNION:** December 3, 1818

OTHER INTERESTING FACTS:

1. Chicago, the largest city in Illinois and the world's greatest inland port, is the only place where the Great Lakes connect with the Mississippi River system. From Chicago you can set out to sail to any port in the world. Ships from opposite ends of the world might pass each other in Chicago's harbor.

2. Barges carry the products of Midwest farms and industries on the Illinois Waterway and the Ohio and Mississippi Rivers: grain, coal, salt, soybeans, ore, petroleum, limestone, and steel. Electric power plants along the river wait for coal. The steel mills wait for coal, limestone, and iron ore. Grain is stored in huge elevators. Much of the cargo will travel to ports to be loaded on ocean-bound ships.

3. More than 75 percent of the land of Illinois is rich, black soil. This rich farmland is the reason young Abraham Lincoln's family was attracted to Illinois. Illinois is as much an energy state as it is a farm state. Much of the state is covered with corn and soybeans—but there is enough coal under this farmland to provide the whole world with coal for an entire century!

SUPER FACT: *Did you know* that the skyscraper was invented in Chicago in the 1880's? It is the strength of a steel frame that makes a skyscraper possible. Chicago's Sears Tower, 110 stories tall, has an observation deck on the 103rd floor. It is the world's tallest building—from it a person can see Wisconsin, Indiana, and Lake Michigan!

ILLINOIS

Unit•At•A•Glance

Read and complete all activities, beginning with **I** and ending with **V**.

I. Language

Draw or paint a picture to show the image that each phrase below brings to your mind; then write two Illinois word images of your own and illustrate them.

• Barges, giant and steady, plowing their way down the Illinois waterways
• Skyscrapers, tall and gaunt, reaching for the heavens

II. Environmental Studies

A stained-glass window is made from many sections of different colors of glass, with designs interwoven to represent a particular idea or mood. Use a black felt-tip pen or crayon to create a stained-glass window design using only geometric shapes. Include as many shapes as you can. Use a variety of colors to show symbols, ideas, scenes, words, and phrases that represent the state of Illinois.

III. Math

List all the shapes used in the stained-glass window. Beside each word listed, draw the shape. Using these shapes only, design a sculpture that could be built to be placed in a museum to represent the state of Illinois. Give your sculpture a title.

IV. Enrichment

Write a short description of your stained-glass window to be used in a travel brochure promoting tourism in Illinois. Be sure to highlight the geometric design, colors used, and featured illustrations. Use the same description to prepare a two-minute radio commercial.

V. Evaluation

Complete the "Illinois Check-Up" worksheet.

ILLINOIS

Decide if the following statements are true or false. Put an "O" beside the true statements and an "X" beside the false statements. (Hint: You will have more X's than O's, so you will want to find the correct answers for every X.)

_____ 1. Chicago is the world's greatest inland port.

_____ 2. Chicago is the only place in North America where the Great Lakes link with the Mississippi River system.

_____ 3. Peoria is the largest city in Illinois.

_____ 4. Barges are no longer used to transport Illinois products.

_____ 5. The violet is the state flower of Illinois.

_____ 6. Cotton is a major crop grown in Illinois.

_____ 7. The Sears Tower in Chicago is the tallest building in the world.

_____ 8. Illinois' supply of coal is almost exhausted.

_____ 9. The "Land of the Famous" is the nickname for Illinois.

_____10. The Cardinal is the state bird of Illinois.

_____11. All the grain produced in Illinois is used in the United States.

INDIANA

The Hoosier State

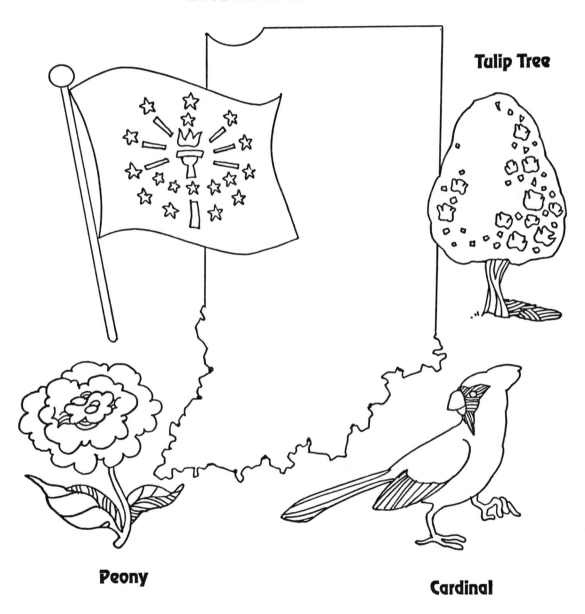

Tulip Tree

Peony

Cardinal

INDIANA

Fact • Sheet

—— FAST FACTS ——

1. **CAPITAL:** Indianapolis

2. **BORDERING STATES:** Kentucky, Illinois, Ohio, Michigan

3. **THREE MAJOR CITIES:** Indianapolis • Fort Wayne • Gary

4. **ADMITTED TO UNION:** December 11, 1816

OTHER INTERESTING FACTS:

1. ❑ Indiana's people seem to have been fascinated with cars for a long, long time. Route 40, one of several broad thoroughfares that make Indiana a crossroads of the nation, was one of the first highways in the United States (in the 1830's it was known as the National Road). And the first automobile with a clutch and an ignition system was invented in 1894 by an Indianan named Elwood Haynes.

2. ❑ Of course the manufacture of automobiles depends on the manufacture of steel. In 1906, the town of Gary, Indiana, was founded—for the sole purpose of manufacturing steel! Today, the town of Gary contains just a fraction of the steel mills, factories, and power plants that line the shore of Lake Michigan. This area is one of the world's most important industrial regions.

3. ❑ Indiana is not all steel mills, factories, and power plants. Corn, wheat, oats, and soybeans that grow on its rich farmland help feed the rest of the world. A large percentage of the soybean crop goes to feed the millions of turkeys raised every year by Indiana farmers.

SUPER FACT: *Did you know* that one theory of the origin of Indiana's nickname (the Hoosier State) is that the response of an early settler to a knock at the door was "Who's Yere?"

Unit•At•A•Glance

Read and complete all activities, beginning with **I** and ending with **V**.

I. Language

Write the script for an imaginary "On the Spot" radio broadcast from Indiana. Tell about the time of year, the weather, and the special event taking place that is worthy of "prime time" radio airing. Use as many descriptive words as you can to make your broadcast interesting, but remember to make the most of your air time by being brief and to the point.

II. Environmental Studies

Pretend that you have been given the responsibility for planning a statewide celebration for Indiana. Write a plan for the celebration, including what you will celebrate, when and how the celebration will take place, and what events will be featured. Plan the celebration so it can be carried out in communities large and small all across the state.

III. Math

Using your list of celebration events, estimate the cost per person for the celebration. Be sure to list the cost of food, games, and souvenirs, plus any special events you have planned. Total all the estimated costs and divide by the number of people expected, to find out how much money each participant would need.

IV. Enrichment

Design, draw, and color a poster to advertise your Indiana celebration. Give special attention to details that would encourage attendance by visitors from outside the state.

V. Evaluation

Complete the "Indiana Check-Up" worksheet.

INDIANA

Check • Up

Find the words in the puzzle to fill in the blanks in the sentences below. You will find the words across, up, and down.

C	I	S	O	Y	B	E	A	N	S	A	B	H
L	G	Y	P	E	O	N	Y	C	D	F	E	O
U	N	S	T	E	E	L	M	G	H	I	J	O
T	I	T	U	K	L	O	I	M	N	O	P	S
C	T	E	R	Q	R	K	C	O	R	N	S	I
H	I	M	K	T	U	I	H	A	V	W	X	E
Y	O	Z	E	A	B	C	I	T	D	E	F	R
G	N	H	Y	I	J	K	G	S	L	M	N	O
P	Q	R	S	W	H	E	A	T	U	V	W	X
Y	Z	A	B	C	D	F	N	G	H	I	J	K
C	A	R	D	I	N	A	L	M	N	O	P	Q

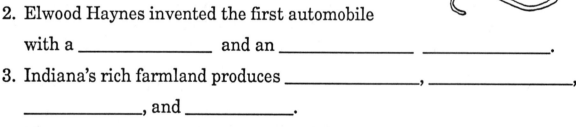

1. The manufacture of automobiles depends on
   the manufacture of _____.
2. Elwood Haynes invented the first automobile
   with a _____ and an _____ _____.
3. Indiana's rich farmland produces _____, _____,
   _____, and _____.
4. The _____ is Indiana's state flower.
5. The city of Gary, Indiana, was built on the shore of Lake _____
   just for the purpose of making steel.
6. Millions of _____ are raised every year by Indiana farmers.
7. Indiana's state bird is the _____.
8. Indiana is known as the _____ state.

MICHIGAN

The Wolverine State

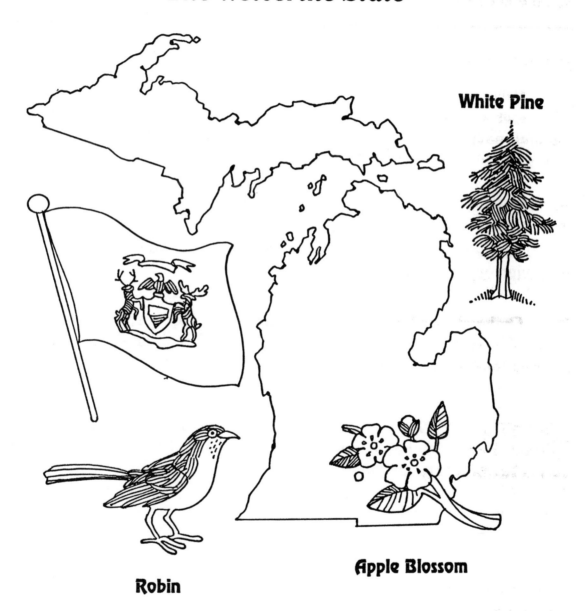

White Pine

Robin

Apple Blossom

MICHIGAN

Fact • Sheet

FAST FACTS

1. **CAPITAL:** Lansing

2. **BORDERING STATES:** Indiana, Ohio, Wisconsin

3. **THREE MAJOR CITIES:** Detroit • Grand Rapids • Warren

4. **ADMITTED TO UNION:** January 26, 1837

OTHER INTERESTING FACTS:

1. Michigan is known as the automobile capital of the nation. More motor vehicles are produced in Michigan than in any other state. The manufacturing associated with truck and car assembly and parts is Michigan's number one industry.

2. Michigan is one of the most popular tourist states in the nation. With shores touching four of the five Great Lakes, and more than 11,000 smaller lakes, Michigan offers beauty and a wide variety of recreation opportunities.

3. Orchards producing cherries, peaches, and apples, along with fields of vegetables, contribute a rich harvest of fresh produce. More sour cherries come from Michigan than from any other state.

SUPER FACT: *Did you know* that four of the five Great Lakes have shorelines in Michigan, and that Michigan is the only mainland state that is two separate sections?

Unit•At•A•Glance

Read and complete all activities, beginning with **I** and ending with **V**.

I. Language

Imagine that you have won the award for being visitor number 1000 to Michigan's Indian Summer celebration. You are to be interviewed on nationwide television about your impression of the state. List the most important topics you will be prepared to discuss.

II. Environmental Studies

Many migrant workers are employed each year to harvest the produce from Michigan's orchards. Write an informational brochure to inform these workers about the state's unique features and its social, educational, and recreational opportunities.

III. Math

This recipe for Sour Cherry Delight will serve six. Recopy the recipe, changing the measurements to make the recipe serve 12 people. Then decide to how many persons you want to serve dessert, figure out the measurements needed, and make Sour Cherry Delight. It's easy and good.

Sour Cherry Delight

1 medium-sized can sour cherries (pitted) • 1 small can crushed pineapple • 2 small packages cherry gelatin • 2 small bottles cola beverage • 1 cup chopped pecans

Drain the cherries and pineapple and reserve the juice. Add enough water to juice to make two cups liquid. Pour into saucepan and heat to boiling. Add gelatin and stir until dissolved. Cool and stir in cola beverage. Pour into mold. Chill until thickened and add fruit and nuts. Chill until firm. Serve with whipped cream.

IV. Enrichment

Pretend that you are a passenger in a hot air balloon. You fly over a vacation community nestled on a secluded Michigan lakefront. Draw or paint a picture of the scene you see below.

V. Evaluation

Complete the "Michigan Check-Up" worksheet.

MICHIGAN

Check•Up

Draw a picture or symbol or write a word or phrase that shows something
from Michigan (flower, bird, natural resource, industry, custom, etc.) in
each box below. It may be hard to think of something for every box,
especially X and Z. Stretch your imagination
and be creative with words, and you will
think of some extraordinary ways to show
off your knowledge of Michigan.

A	B		
C	D	E	F
G	H	I	J
K	L	M	N
O	P	Q	R
S	T	U	V
W	X	Y	Z

OHIO

The Buckeye State

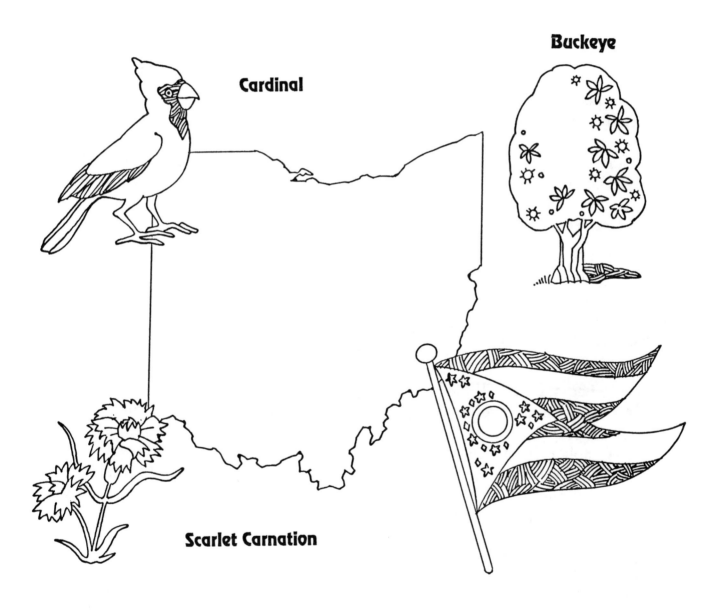

Cardinal

Buckeye

Scarlet Carnation

OHIO

Fact • Sheet

```
┌─────────────────────────────────── FAST FACTS ───┐
│  1. CAPITAL: Columbus                              │
│                                                    │
│  2. BORDERING STATES: Michigan, Indiana, Kentucky, West Virginia, │
│  Pennsylvania                                      │
│                                                    │
│  3. THREE MAJOR CITIES: Columbus • Cleveland • Cincinnati │
│                                                    │
│  4. ADMITTED TO UNION: March 1, 1803               │
└────────────────────────────────────────────────────┘
```

OTHER INTERESTING FACTS:

1. Sometimes people call Ohio "the most American state." Ohio does seem to contain pieces of many other parts of America. Its northeast corner has a bit of the flavor of New England—many of its villages were settled originally by New Englanders. Western Ohio is farm country, filled with farmers' markets and grain elevators. The hills of southeastern Ohio gave rise to coal mining towns. Long ago, Polish and German immigrants settled in Cincinnati; some people think parts of the city have the feel of old New York.

2. The Ohio River has played a key role in the growth of the city of Cincinnati. This river bears a tremendous amount of traffic, both passenger and commercial—even more than the St. Lawrence Seaway or the Panama Canal! Cincinnati lies between West Virginia's coalfields and Kentucky's coalfields; it should come as no surprise to learn that this city is the largest inland coal distribution center in the world.

3. Legend has it that Johnny Appleseed traveled on foot through central Ohio, planting apple seeds as he wandered. The legend is true! Johnny Appleseed (whose real name was John Chapman) planted all these apple trees because of his religious faith: he believed that he was called to plant trees so that frontier families would have access to fresh fruit. Beginning in 1801, Johnny Appleseed acquired seeds from Pennsylvania cider presses, carried them to Ohio, and spent almost 40 years looking for good spots to plant apple trees.

SUPER FACT: *Did you know* that two men who performed important space "firsts" were from Ohio? John Glenn was the first American to orbit in space, and Neil Armstrong was the first man to step onto the moon. (Also, workers in Akron, Ohio, made the first space suits for American astronauts.)

OHIO

Unit•At•A•Glance

Read and complete all activities, beginning with **I** and ending with **V.**

I. Language

Explain the difference between a tall tale, a myth, and a legend. Tell which definition you think best fits the well-known story about Johnny Appleseed. Write a tall tale, myth, or legend about why the Cardinal was named the state bird of Ohio.

II. Environmental Studies

Write the names of Ohio's three major cities. Compare and contrast the climate, geography, and major industries of the three. Place a star beside the city in which you would most like to live. Write a paragraph of not more than four sentences to explain your choice.

III. Math

Draw a color-by-number picture of an Ohio grain elevator, using four colors and numbering them with even numbers between 4 and 16. Ask a friend to follow the numbers to color the picture and then to identify it.

IV. Enrichment

Draw and color a sequence of four pictures to show four stages of an Ohio apple tree's growth from seedling to fruit production. Write a brief story to go with your pictures, design a cover, and staple or hole-punch and tie your work together to make a booklet.

V. Evaluation

Complete the "Ohio Check-Up" worksheet.

OHIO

Check•Up

Draw lines from the words or phrases
to the matching picture symbols.
On the lines below, write a sentence
or phrase to tell how each word or
phrase relates to the state of Ohio.

1. Johnny Appleseed
2. grain elevator
3. Ohio River
4. barge
5. coal
6. Scarlet Carnation
7. Cardinal
8. buckeye
9. factories
10. grain fields
11. farmers' market
12. space suit

1. _____
2. _____
3. _____
4. _____
5. _____
6. _____
7. _____
8. _____
9. _____
10. _____
11. _____
12. _____

WISCONSIN

The Badger State

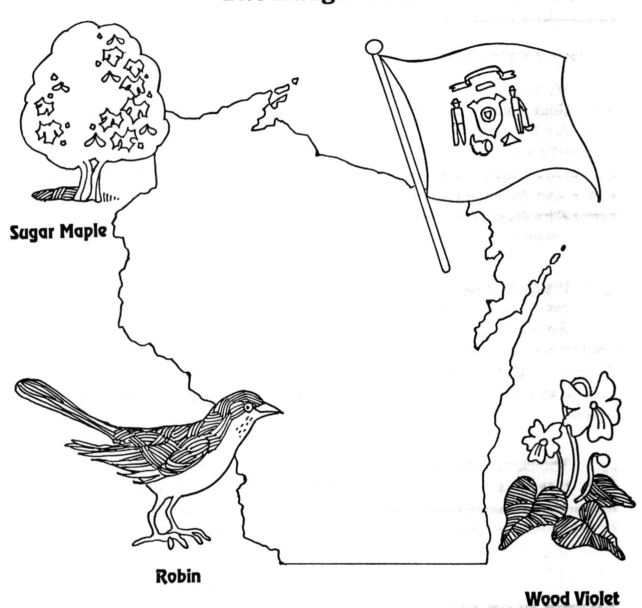

Sugar Maple

Robin

Wood Violet

WISCONSIN

Fact • Sheet

FAST FACTS

1. **CAPITAL:** Madison

2. **BORDERING STATES:** Minnesota, Iowa, Illinois, Michigan

3. **THREE MAJOR CITIES:** Milwaukee • Madison • Green Bay

4. **ADMITTED TO UNION:** May 29, 1848

OTHER INTERESTING FACTS:

1. ❑ Wisconsin had a Lead Boom in the 1830's and 1840's. This was like a Gold Rush in that people streamed into the state to take advantage of the country's need for paint and ammunition (lead is used in the manufacture of both of these products). Some miners didn't bother to build houses, but lived in caves or in the mines themselves. Some thought these people were behaving like badgers, burrowing into the ground: thus Wisconsin's nickname, "The Badger State"! Most of the lead was gone by 1850, and most of the miners left. Those who stayed became farmers.

2. ❑ It was William Hoard, a newspaperman who was later elected governor, who is given credit for the transformation of Wisconsin into "America's Dairyland." In 1870 he began to promote his idea that dairy farming was the best way for Wisconsin farmers to make money. Each year Wisconsin's 2 million dairy cows produce enough milk to supply 42 million persons, enough butter for 68 million persons, and cheese for 86 million persons.

3. ❑ Thousands of years ago, glaciers carved out low places in what is now Wisconsin. When the glaciers melted for the last time, they left behind thousands of lakes. Lake Winnebago is the largest, covering 215 square miles. Its beaches are tremendous tourist attractions, with swimming, motorboating, and sailing.

SUPER FACT: *Did you know* that five Ringling Brothers started their famous circus in Baraboo, Wisconsin, in 1884?

WISCONSIN

Unit•At•A•Glance

Read and complete all activities, beginning with **I** and ending with **V**.

I. Language

Write a "State of the State" speech that the governor of Wisconsin might make at a National Governor's Conference to report on the state's progress and outlook for the future. Follow this procedure:
(1) List important facts and ideas that need to be included.
(2) Write the speech.
(3) Make cue cards to be used during the presentation.

II. Environmental Studies

Using this riddle as a "starter," write three science or social studies riddles about Wisconsin's natural resources: "I am a small, four-legged animal who burrows underground. My name is also Wisconsin's nickname. What is my name?" (Answer: Badger.) Ask a friend to solve your riddles.

III. Math

Create three math word-story problems based on Wisconsin's dairy industry. Use liquid measurement in one, linear measurement in one, and metric measurement in the third. Ask a friend to solve your problems. Check the answers.

IV. Enrichment

Make a three-dimensional collage of junk from your desk, pockets, backpack, or whatever you have at hand, to represent some important feature of Wisconsin (natural resources, symbols, history, landscape, etc.). You might use paper scraps, crayon bits, coins, paper clips, etc.

V. Evaluation

Complete the "Wisconsin Check-Up" worksheet.

WISCONSIN

Check•Up

Pretend that you have a magic carpet that will let you fly over the state of Wisconsin. Trace your travels on the map below as you see Wisconsin from the air. Add and label the state capital, major cities, rivers, mountains, seashore, and other geographical features. Add the state flower, tree, bird, and other unique features.

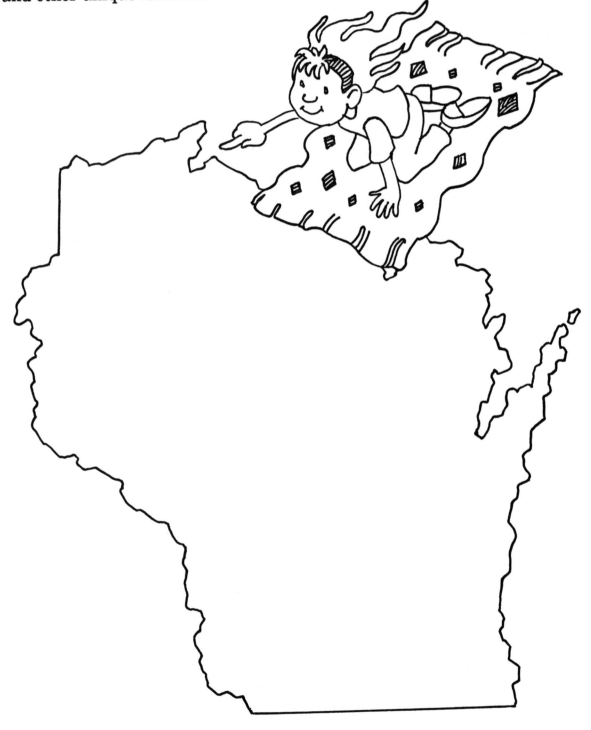

The Midwest

North Dakota

Minnesota

South Dakota

Iowa

Nebraska

Kansas

Missouri

IOWA

The Hawkeye State

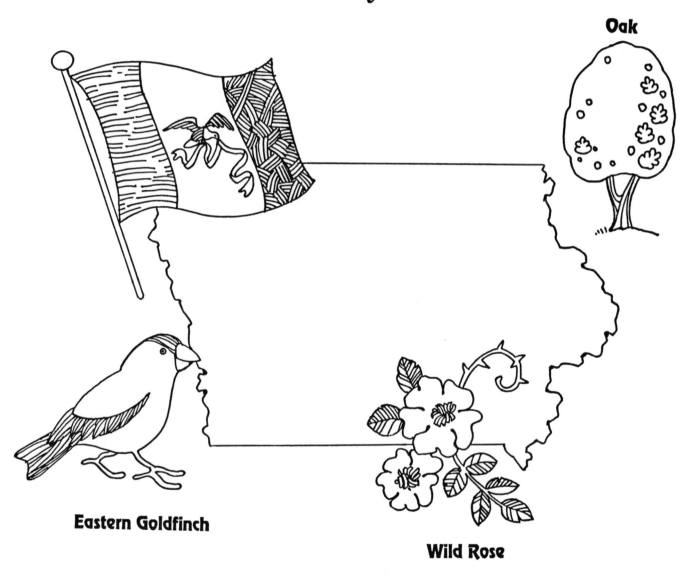

Oak

Eastern Goldfinch

Wild Rose

IOWA

Fact • Sheet

OTHER INTERESTING FACTS:

1. ☐ The great Missouri River runs along Iowa's western border, and the Mississippi River runs along its eastern border. Most of the land in the state is rather flat, but there are hills forested with oak, maple, and birch trees that ascend from the river valleys; for this reason, northeastern Iowa is sometimes called "Little Switzerland."

2. ☐ Before farmers cultivated the plains of Iowa, the land was covered with grassy fields that stretched from horizon to horizon. When farmers began to settle these plains, corn gradually replaced the wild grasses—sometimes people jokingly call Iowa "the biggest cornfield on Earth!" But people come from near and far to visit Iowa's universities, seed houses, plant nurseries, and farms. Agriculturalists of the state are constantly working on the development of improved feed for livestock, improved corn crops—even improved breeds of animals!

3. ☐ Don't think that corn is Iowa's only product! The town of Muscatine, Iowa, grew when people found they could make buttons from clam shells found in the river. The buttons looked like pearl buttons, the demand for them grew—and button factories sprang up in Muscatine. Dubuque, Iowa, came into being because its land was the location of lead mines, and it continues to produce lead today.

SUPER FACT: *Did you know* that the home of the largest popcorn factory in the United States is Sioux City, Iowa? Popcorn is made when a special kind of corn kernel with a hard coating is heated. The kernel explodes when the heat turns its trapped moisture into steam. A fluffy piece of popcorn is many times larger than the original kernel—sometimes as much as 35 times larger!

Unit•At•A•Glance

Read and complete all activities, beginning with **I** and ending with **V.**

I. Language

List five natural resources and/or industries of Iowa. Beside each resource, list two adjectives to describe it. Reread your list and try to replace as many of the adjectives as you can with more interesting descriptive words.

II. Environmental Studies

Make a series of pencil sketches to show the stages that popcorn goes through from raw kernel to "edible" popcorn. Begin with the unshelled corn still on the cob and end with a "popped right, ready to pop into your mouth" morsel. Make a list of six ways popcorn can be used (holiday decorations, bird food, etc.).

III. Math

Draw a time line to show the development of Iowa's vast farming industry, from grass fields to high-tech farms and farm-related industries.

IV. Enrichment

Create a brand-new, never-before-thought-of use for Iowa corn shucks. Draw a detailed sketch of the product. Write a description of it and tell how, where, and by whom it would be produced and used.

V. Evaluation

Complete the "Iowa Check-Up" worksheet.

IOWA

Check•Up

Pretend that you have been selected to create a museum display to represent Iowa. Select a theme for your display, sketch your display, and label each item. Be sure to include the state symbols, natural resources, and industries, as well as interesting facts related to the state's history and culture.

Theme: _____

KANSAS

The Sunflower State

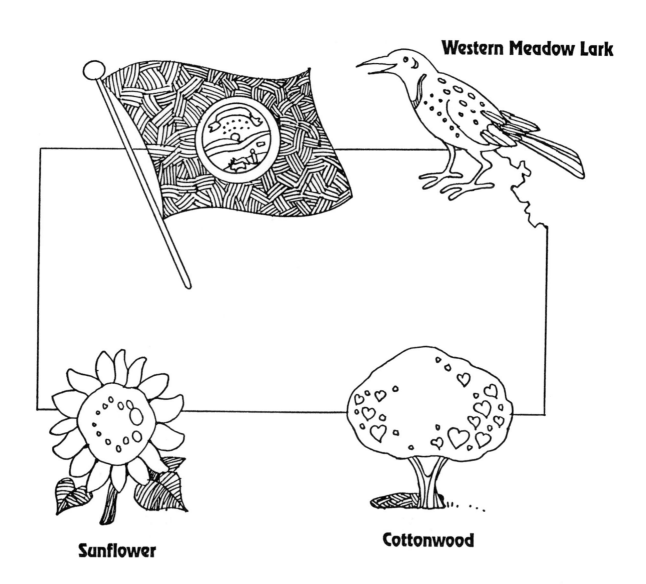

Western Meadow Lark

Sunflower

Cottonwood

KANSAS

Fact • Sheet

FAST FACTS

1. **CAPITAL:** Topeka

2. **BORDERING STATES:** Missouri, Oklahoma, Colorado, Nebraska

3. **THREE MAJOR CITIES:** Wichita • Kansas City • Topeka

4. **ADMITTED TO UNION:** January 29, 1861

OTHER INTERESTING FACTS:

1. Kansas wheat fields stretch as far as the eye can see. At one time these fields were desert, and it was thought that crops could not grow here because of the lack of rain. Then Russian settlers of Kansas brought seeds of hard red winter wheat, which grows very well in places of little rainfall. The hard wheat now grows in an area that runs from Texas into Nebraska.

2. Wheat-harvesting is the nation's biggest food-gathering operation. Caravans of trucks carrying combines travel up to Kansas from Texas in early summer and move from one huge wheat farm to another. Harvesting crews work long, hard hours, even through the night, to cut the wheat, because the crop is vulnerable to destruction by sudden changes in weather. When the wheat is cut, the combines thresh the grain from the stalks. The grain is loaded onto trucks which carry it to storage places in nearby towns.

3. Abilene, Dodge City, and Wichita were once known as "cow towns." In the late 1800's, Texas cowboys would herd longhorn cattle to Kansas rail stops. When railroads were built to connect Texas with the eastern United States, this practice died down—but the "cow towns" remained, to become cities with factories that build planes, missiles, parts for jets, camping equipment, refining oil, and processing grain.

SUPER FACT: *Did you know* that the elevators in which grain is stored are so tall that they are nicknamed "prairie cathedrals"?

Unit•At•A•Glance

Read and complete all activities, beginning with **I** and ending with **V**.

I. Language

Write a creative story based on how
life would have been different for
early citizens of Kansas if the Russian
immigrants had not brought hard red
winter wheat seeds from the homes they had left across the sea.

II. Environmental Studies

Do a little farming on your own to help you learn more
about growing sunflowers. Wash and dry a cut-off milk
carton or cottage cheese container (not plastic) to
make a planter. Fill it with loose soil and plant 3 to 5
sunflower seeds. Place your planter in a sunny
window. Water it just enough to keep the soil moist
and wait for your seeds to sprout and grow. Keep a
chart of the plants' growth. When the plants are
sturdy enough, plant them outside. If you raise these
plants to bloom, you'll have done the wild birds in your neighborhood a big
favor. If you can't get sunflower seeds, draw a series of four pictures to
show the growth cycle of a sunflower from seed to flower.

III. Math

List three times during the year that estimation skills would be important
to wheat farmers in Kansas. Beside each time, write one
sentence to tell how estimation skills would be used.

IV. Enrichment

Draw or paint a field of sunflowers in full bloom or
golden wheat fields ready for harvest. Write an original
poem, jingle, or legend based on your artistic creation.

V. Evaluation

Complete the "Kansas Check-Up" worksheet.

KANSAS

Design a "Welcome to Kansas" billboard that includes a warm welcoming message, pictures of the state flag, bird, tree and flower, and any other special features that would tell a visitor about the state.

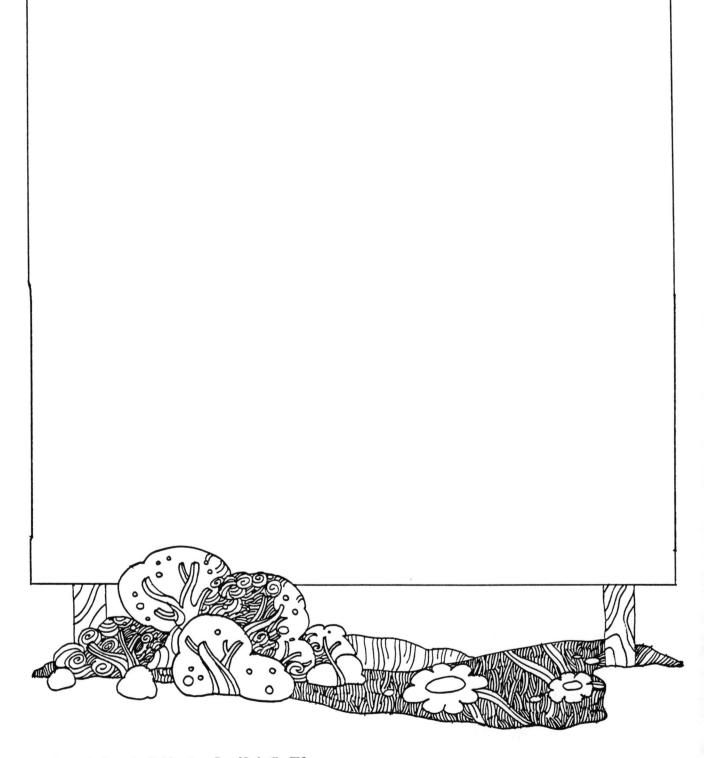

MINNESOTA

The Gopher State

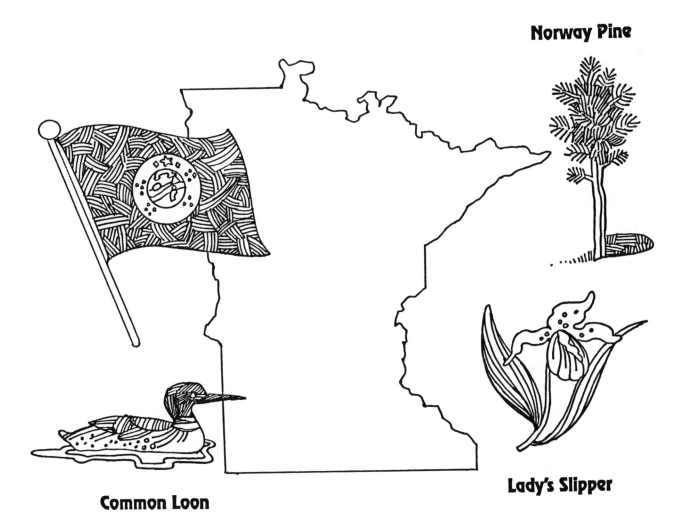

Norway Pine

Common Loon

Lady's Slipper

MINNESOTA

Fact • Sheet

┌─────────────────────────────────────── **FAST FACTS** ───┐

1. **CAPITAL:** St. Paul

2. **BORDERING STATES:** North Dakota, South Dakota, Iowa, Wisconsin

3. **THREE MAJOR CITIES:** Minneapolis • St. Paul • Bloomington

4. **ADMITTED TO UNION:** May 11, 1858

└──┘

OTHER INTERESTING FACTS:

1. Minnesotans sometimes refer to their state as the Land of 10,000 Lakes. There are actually more than 15,000 lakes located in this state. Many of the lakes were formed long ago by glaciers. Small lakes called "kettle holes" were formed when huge chunks of ice that had gotten trapped in layers of debris finally melted. One of the nation's major ports, Duluth, is located on Lake Superior. Freighters carry grain, iron ore, and manufactured goods to other cities on the Great Lakes and to ports overseas.

2. Minnesota's most valuable resource is its soil. It, too, is a result of glacier activity long ago. Glaciers carried into the region fine-ground stone called "drift." Drift is a component of rich soil. Minnesota grows corn and oats, much of which go to feed its beef cattle and dairy cows. The milk from its one million dairy cows is used to produce butter.

3. Early Native Americans cherished an unusual red stone that is found in Southwest Minnesota. The Native Americans carved peace pipes, known as calumets, from this stone. It is said that even enemies remained peaceful when they visited the site from which came this stone, for the site was thought to be sacred. It is now known as Pipestone National Monument, and is made up of 160 acres of prairie that has not changed much in several centuries.

SUPER FACT: *Did you know* that Minnesota raises more turkeys than does any other state in the Union? Benjamin Franklin pushed unsuccessfully to have this native bird named our national symbol.

140

Unit•At•A•Glance

Read and complete all activities, beginning with **I** and ending with **V**.

I. Language

In honor of the millions of turkeys raised in
Minnesota each year, use one of the story
starters below as the theme for a creative story:
• There it was, a two hundred pound turkey...
• Turkeys, turkeys, turkeys...
• As far as we know, Tanya is the world's first
  talking turkey...
• Ever since this turkey won first prize at the Minnesota state fair...

II. Environmental Studies

Minnesota is one of the nation's "food
basket" states. Make a list of everything
you ate yesterday. Put a star beside all
the foods that could have come from this
state. Design a poster with a slogan to
help protect this plant or animal.

III. Math

Using the list of foods you ate yesterday, compute the cost of each item
according to your best estimate. Then add up the costs to find out how
much your food for the day cost.

IV. Enrichment

Pretend you have inherited a lakefront lot on
one of Minnesota's beautiful lakes. Think about
how you would want to spend your vacations
there. Design a vacation home that you would
build. Draw the plan and tell how you would
furnish the house and what special recreational equipment you would need.

V. Evaluation

Complete the "Minnesota Check-Up" worksheet.

MINNESOTA

Check•Up

Write an entry on Minnesota for a textbook entitled "America, The Fifty Great States." The guidelines are:

1. Only factual and current information may be used.
2. The article must be limited to one handwritten page and must contain as many facts and as much interesting information as possible.

Include state symbols, occupations, industries, and geographical features.

MISSOURI

The Show Me State

Hawthorn

Bluebird

Flowering Dogwood

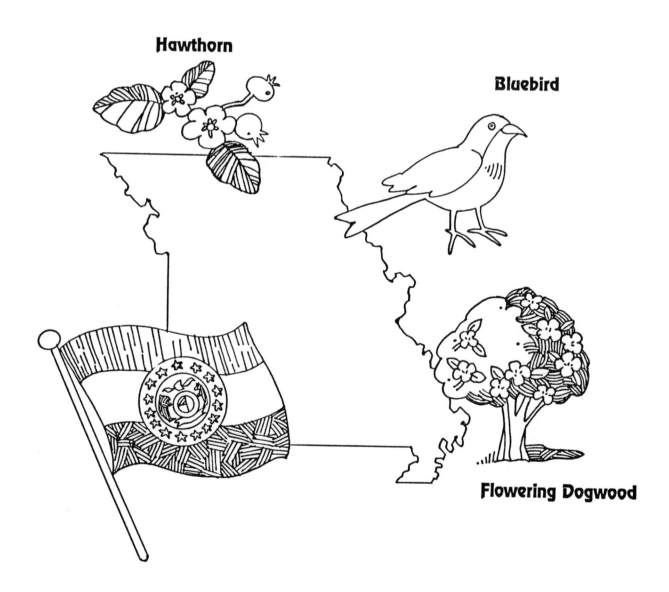

MISSOURI

Fact • Sheet

FAST FACTS

1. **CAPITAL:** Jefferson City

2. **BORDERING STATES:** Illinois, Kentucky, Tennessee, Arkansas, Oklahoma, Kansas, Nebraska, Iowa

3. **THREE MAJOR CITIES:** Kansas City • St. Louis • Springfield

4. **ADMITTED TO UNION:** August 10, 1821

OTHER INTERESTING FACTS:

1. ❑ You may have seen pictures of St. Louis's famous Gateway Arch. Did you know that it rises more than 600 feet above the ground? Did you know that more than 900 tons of stainless steel were used to form its outer covering? It is the nation's tallest man-made monument. And it was built as a symbol of St. Louis's fame as the "Gateway to the West." This means that thousands of pioneers traveled to St. Louis from the East, then spread out to lands in the West.

2. ❑ Northern Missouri has much farmland, and its farmers grow soybeans and corn. Farther south is the Ozark Plateau, an interesting configuration of caves and river valleys that make the mountains seem higher than they really are in comparison to sea level. Some of the caves formed by the underground streams are so large they could be used as underground parking lots!

3. ❑ Missouri is known for its crafts festivals, which keep alive the native crafts traditions. If you visit some of these festivals, you will be able to see glassblowers, broom makers, potters, chair makers, weavers, cornhusk-dollmakers, and makers of corncob pipes. The corncob pipe is one of the trademarks of Missouri, and pipes are turned out by the thousand by factory workers in Washington, Missouri.

SUPER FACT: *Did you know* that the famous Pony Express was begun in St. Joseph, Missouri, in 1860?

Unit•At•A•Glance

Read and complete all activities, beginning with **I** and ending with **V.**

I. Language

Pretend that you are a Pony Express rider. Write a story about some of your adventures. Use 1860 as the time of your story, and Missouri as the setting.

II. Environmental Studies

Compare and contrast the advantages and disadvantages of the daily life of a resident of the bustling city of St. Louis with those of a resident in the rugged hills of the Ozark region.

III. Math

Construct a time line to show the development of transportation in Missouri from the early days of the Pony Express to today's super highways and jet planes.

IV. Enrichment

Use your Pony Express adventure story as the theme for a TV mini-series. Outline the plot, sequence of events, and cast of characters. Provide sketches of costumes and sets.

V. Evaluation

Complete the "Missouri Check-Up" worksheet.

MISSOURI

Check•Up

Make a list of ten good questions that you would ask to help another person learn about Missouri. Be sure to include questions about state symbols, natural resources, and other features of interest. First, write all your questions, then write answers. Finally, select someone to be your student!

Questions   Answers

1. _____   1. _____

2. _____   2. _____

3. _____   3. _____

4. _____   4. _____

5. _____   5. _____

6. _____   6. _____

7. _____   7. _____

8. _____   8. _____

9. _____   9. _____

10. _____   10. _____

NEBRASKA

The Cornhusker State

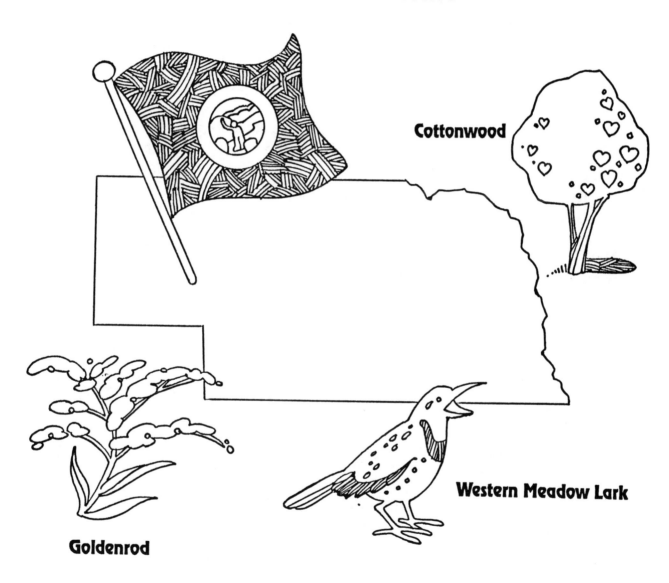

Cottonwood

Goldenrod

Western Meadow Lark

NEBRASKA

Fact • Sheet

```
┌─────────────────────────────────────── FAST FACTS ───┐
│                                                        │
│  1. CAPITAL: Lincoln                                   │
│                                                        │
│  2. BORDERING STATES: Kansas, Colorado, Wyoming,       │
│     South Dakota, Iowa, Missouri                       │
│                                                        │
│  3. THREE MAJOR CITIES: Omaha • Lincoln • Grand Island │
│                                                        │
│  4. ADMITTED TO UNION: March 1, 1867                   │
│                                                        │
└────────────────────────────────────────────────────────┘
```

OTHER INTERESTING FACTS:

1. Archeologists have found evidence to indicate that prehistoric people hunted big game more than 10,000 years ago in the area that is now the state of Nebraska. They were followed by tribes who raised corn, vegetables, and sunflowers. Many of these Native Americans were still living in Nebraska when the first European explorers and fur traders arrived in the 1700's. Descendants of these early tribes still live in Nebraska and contribute greatly to its culture and lifestyle. They lead modern lives but are encouraged by governing tribal councils to remember and honor old customs and traditions.

2. Located near the center of the nation, Nebraska has a steady flow of traffic from border to border of the state. The railroad system, which played an important role in the early development of the state, is still very active, and so are a superhighway system, intra-state bus lines, and over 100 airports.

3. Agriculture is the most important industry in Nebraska due to fertile soil, abundance of ground water, and favorable climate. The state ranks first in the production of Great Northern beans, second in livestock slaughter, third in corn production, and sixth in the production of honey.

SUPER FACT: *Did you know* that Interstate 80, which runs the entire length of Nebraska, is the most traveled transcontinental highway in the United States?

NEBRASKA

Unit•At•A•Glance

Read and complete all activities, beginning with **I** and ending with **V**.

I. Language

Choose one of Nebraska's two nicknames, "The Cornhusker State" or "The Tree Planter State," as the most representative of the state. Then write a letter addressed to the Governor of Nebraska supporting your choice.

II. Environmental Studies

List three specific ways weather forecasts are important to farmers in Nebraska. Write a paragraph telling how the agricultural industry would be affected if there were no weather predictions and/or information available for a three month period (use either spring, summer, winter, or fall).

III. Math

Write four word problems about Nebraska that will be solved by subtraction. Solve the problems and tell if each "difference" is an odd or even number.

IV. Enrichment

Since so many people travel Nebraska's highways en route to a destination outside the state, design three roadside signs:
- One to welcome motorists to the state;
- One to invite travelers to slow down and stay awhile; and
- One to invite motorists to "come again."

V. Evaluation

Complete the "Nebraska Check-Up" worksheet.

NEBRASKA

Check • Up

Add pictures, symbols, words, and phrases to the wreath below to "tell the world" about Nebraska. Add a big bow and tell where the wreath should be hung.

NORTH DAKOTA

The Flickertail State

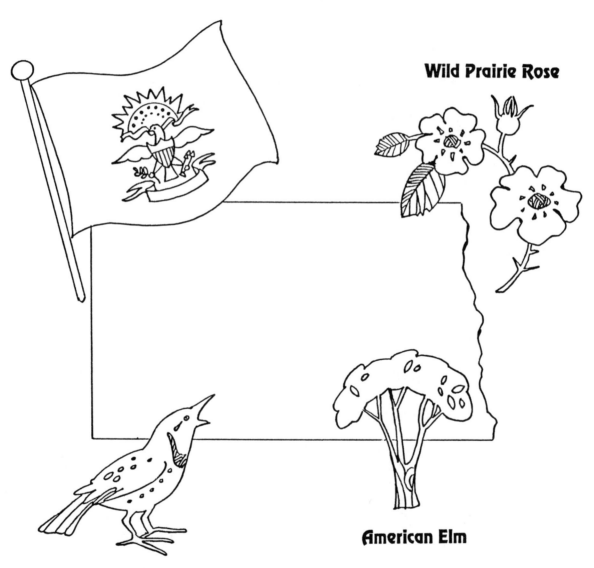

Wild Prairie Rose

American Elm

Western Meadow Lark

NORTH DAKOTA

Fact • Sheet

1. **CAPITAL:** Bismarck

2. **BORDERING STATES:** Montana, South Dakota, Minnesota

3. **THREE MAJOR CITIES:** Fargo • Grand Forks • Bismarck

4. **ADMITTED TO UNION:** November 2, 1889

OTHER INTERESTING FACTS:

1. North Dakota is famous for its severe, bleak winters. It also has very hot summers. This is what is known as a "continental" climate, which occurs in locations that have no large bodies of water. (Bodies of water such as large lakes and the sea tend to soften extremes of climate so that winters and summers are milder.) In spite of these extremes of climate, no other state in America relies so much on agriculture. More sunflowers, spring wheat, barley, rye, pinto beans, and flax are grown in North Dakota than in any other state. (Flax is used to make linen and linseed oil.) Because the state is so far north, the hours of summer sunshine are long ones, which means that plants grow rapidly.

2. The early North Dakota settlers found treeless, grassy plains. With very little wood to use for building houses and barns, they resourcefully invented the "soddie"—a house, shed, or barn made from heavy slices of earth and grass. Houses of sod were warm in the winter and cool in the summer. Of course, they could leak terribly during a heavy rainstorm, and insects could cause problems, too!

3. Western North Dakota is a source of oil, and has the world's largest deposits of lignite, a brownish-black coal. Lignite is mined by operators of huge machines that can extract a single hunk of earth the size of a small building all at once. Other midwestern states purchase much of the electrical power that is manufactured by burning this coal.

SUPER FACT: *Did you know* that the geographic center of the North American continent is in North Dakota? It is near Rugby, and is 1500 miles from the Atlantic, Pacific, and Arctic Oceans and from the Gulf of Mexico.

NORTH DAKOTA

Unit•At•A•Glance

Read and complete all activities, beginning with **I** and ending with **V**.

I. Language

Use one of the following story starters as the theme of a creative story. Imagine you are writing this story to be included in an anthology of stories about the plains and prairies of North Dakota.
• Fields of sunflowers appear to stretch endlessly across the plains...
• Living in a sod house in winter had its drawbacks...
• Coal, the black gold of North Dakota...
• A North Dakota weather forecaster's worst nightmare...

II. Environmental Studies

North Dakota is a state of harsh winters and hot summers. Write three questions related to the weather that a company executive considering relocating a business to North Dakota would want answered before making a final decision. Use reference materials to find answers for your questions.

III. Math

Make up three math word problems with themes related to North Dakota. Write each problem on one index card and each answer on another (you will need six cards in all). Ask a friend to check your answers.

IV. Enrichment

Design a modern-day home, comparable to the sod homes of early times in that it would be built from grass and soil, but differing in that it would be reinforced with steel, concrete, or other foundation materials. List advantages and disadvantages of this type of home for homeowners of today.

V. Evaluation

Complete the "North Dakota Check-Up" worksheet.

NORTH DAKOTA

Check • Up

Write ten questions and answers for a North Dakota Trivia Game. Use all the words in the word box to help you cover the important facts about the state.

flax	soddies	tree	Fargo
continental climate	oil	bird	Bismarck
grass	coal	nickname	Grand Forks
weather extremes	flower	capital city	Rugby

Questions

1. _____

2. _____

3. _____

4. _____

5. _____

6. _____

7. _____

8. _____

9. _____

10. _____

Answers

1. _____

2. _____

3. _____

4. _____

5. _____

6. _____

7. _____

8. _____

9. _____

10. _____

SOUTH DAKOTA

The Sunshine State

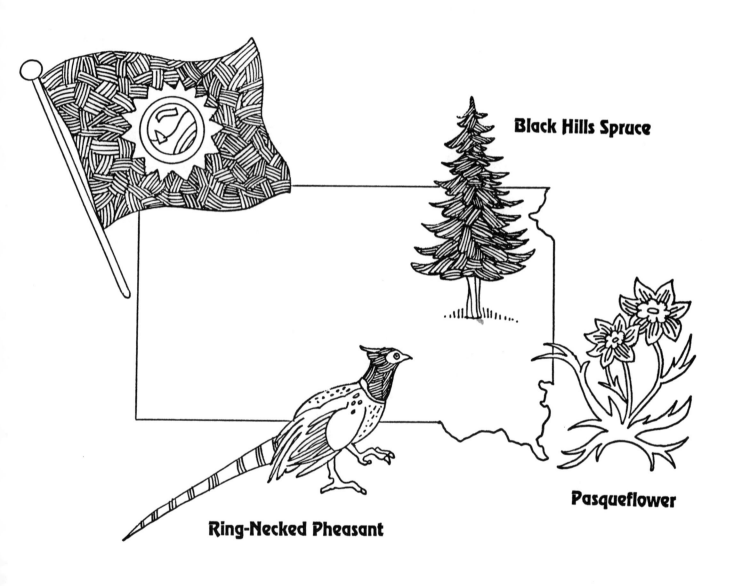

Black Hills Spruce

Pasqueflower

Ring-Necked Pheasant

SOUTH DAKOTA

Fact • Sheet

FAST FACTS

1. **CAPITAL:** Pierre

2. **BORDERING STATES:** North Dakota, Minnesota, Iowa, Nebraska, Wyoming, Montana

3. **THREE MAJOR CITIES:** Sioux Falls • Rapid City • Aberdeen

4. **ADMITTED TO UNION:** November 2, 1889

OTHER INTERESTING FACTS:

1. Think of a western movie you have seen. Chances are good that you were watching a film made in South Dakota! This state has all the necessary ingredients: gold mines, ghost towns, wild rivers for pioneers to cross, prairies to provide homes for buffalo, and mountain passes that are good hiding places for outlaws. And in this state are the Black Hills, which are really small mountains that got their name from the Sioux. From the plains, the hills looked black because of the pine and spruce trees that covered them.

2. In 1874, people rushed into the Black Hills because news of the discovery of gold had spread. The Black Hills were sacred to the Sioux, and they fought the prospectors. Gold is still mined in the Black Hills. From each ton of gold ore comes a fifth of an ounce of gold!

3. Mount Rushmore, a remarkable tribute to American leaders who fought for freedom, was begun in 1927 by Gutzon Borglum. He and his crew worked 14 years to carve the faces of George Washington, Thomas Jefferson, Abraham Lincoln, and Theodore Roosevelt. Their "sculpting" of the hard mountain rock was accomplished with the use of dynamite!

SUPER FACT: *Did you know* that the American gold mine that produces more gold than any other in America is the Homestake Gold Mine in the town of Lead, South Dakota?

Unit•At•A•Glance

Read and complete all activities, beginning with **I** and ending with **V**.

I. Language

South Dakota has been the scene of
many of America's western films. Using
the mountains, raging streams, and vast
prairies as a backdrop, write the script
for a modern "wild west" film. Don't
forget to include a villain and a victor
and lots of excitement.

II. Environmental Studies

Think of the one American hero you would add to the four honored on
Mount Rushmore, and write a
paragraph supporting your
choice.

III. Math

Develop a budget for the
production of your film. Let
your imagination soar, but
start with a figure of no more
than $70,000 and no less than
$17,000. High or low budget, the decision is yours, but list all estimated
costs and be sure you end with a balanced
budget.

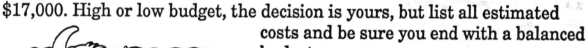

IV. Enrichment

Draw or paint a background scene to be
used for your western film.

V. Evaluation

Complete the "South Dakota Check-Up"
worksheet.

SOUTH DAKOTA

Check•Up

Complete the design for an original weaving to communicate the color and spirit of South Dakota. Include the state bird, tree, flag, and flower, the Black Hills, Sioux, Mt. Rushmore, buffalo, gold mines, ghost towns, and other important elements.

The Southwest

Arizona

New Mexico

Oklahoma

Texas

ARIZONA

The Grand Canyon State

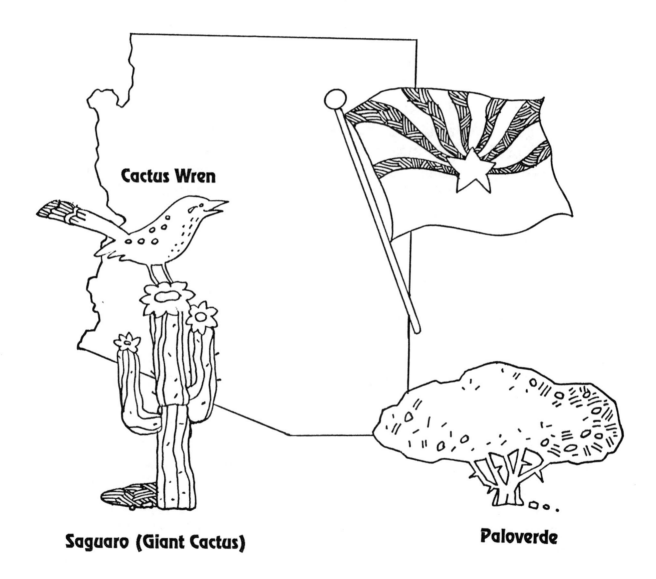

Cactus Wren

Saguaro (Giant Cactus)

Paloverde

ARIZONA

Fact • Sheet

1. **CAPITAL:** Phoenix

2. **BORDERING STATES:** California, Nevada, Utah, New Mexico, Colorado

3. **THREE MAJOR CITIES:** Phoenix • Tucson • Mesa

4. **ADMITTED TO UNION:** February 14, 1912

OTHER INTERESTING FACTS:

1. ❑ The Petrified Forest National Park, located between Gallup and Flagstaff, Arizona, is a rich resource for scientists studying fossils for clues to prehistoric times. Trees were covered here by mud and sand and, since oxygen was scarce, they remained in a decayed state. Water containing silica seeped into them and the silica crystallized into quartz. Oxides of manganese and iron are responsible for the vivid colors to be observed in the park today.

2. ❑ A scarcity of water is one of Arizona's greatest problems today. As Arizona's cities, towns, and even outlying desert and mountain areas have become more heavily populated, the rainfall has simply not been adequate to supply the water necessary for day-to-day consumption. Researchers are devising and studying plans for piping water from the Colorado River. Meanwhile, the problem of Arizona's water supply remains uppermost in the minds of its citizens.

3. ❑ Life for Arizona's early settlers was not easy. The intense climate, rugged mountains, desert snakes and other dangerous wildlife, and hostile Apache warriors made it very difficult for early explorers to settle Arizona's wildlands. It was the quest for gold and silver that finally encouraged permanent settlements to spring up in what is now the state of Arizona.

SUPER FACT: *Did you know* that half the copper produced in the United States is produced in Arizona?

Unit•At•A•Glance

Read and complete all activities, beginning with **I** and ending with **V**.

I. Language

Write a diamond-shaped poem about the
deserts of Arizona. Use the following form:

Noun
Two words describing the noun
Three words ending in -ed or -ing
Four words ending in -ed or -ing
Three words ending in -ed or -ing
Two words describing the noun
Noun

II. Environmental Studies

Think about how Arizona's water shortage affects the lives of people there,
and then think about how a water shortage would affect people in your
state. List ten things people in your state could do to conserve water. Tell
how this would affect day-to-day life. (If you live in Arizona, write about
what Arizonans have done to conserve water.)

III. Math

Ask six people to answer the following question: "Do you think water
should be rationed in Arizona today?" Graph your findings,
then write a newspaper article presenting your findings.

IV. Enrichment

Fold a sheet of drawing paper into three equal parts. Label
the sections (1) Plants, (2) Animals, and (3) Occupations
(one topic for each section). Draw or paint pictures to show ten items
related to each sub-
ject. Unfold your com-
pleted mural and dis-
cuss it with a friend.

V. Evaluation

Complete the
"Arizona Check-Up"
worksheet.

ARIZONA

Fill the space below with words, pictures, and symbols to show artifacts that you would place in a time capsule to leave for people one hundred years from now who might want to learn what Arizona was like in the twentieth century. Don't forget to include the flag, flower, bird, natural resources, occupations, capital, customs, etc.

NEW MEXICO

The Land Of Enchantment

Nut Pine

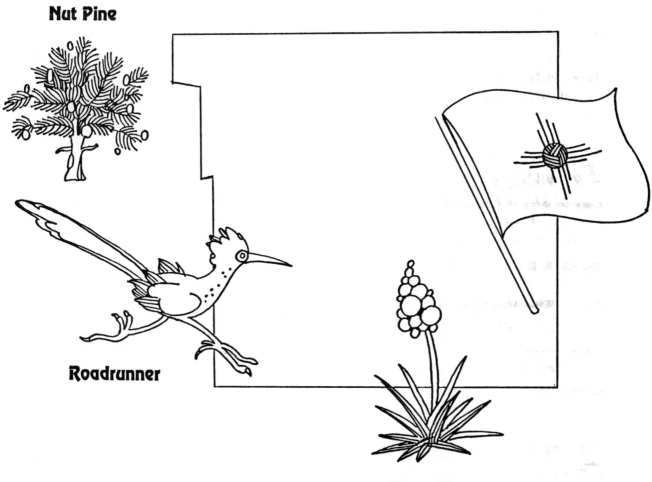

Roadrunner

Yucca Flower

NEW MEXICO

Fact • Sheet

FAST FACTS

1. **CAPITAL:** Santa Fe

2. **BORDERING STATES:** Arizona, Colorado, Oklahoma, Texas

3. **THREE MAJOR CITIES:** Albuquerque • Santa Fe • Las Cruces

4. **ADMITTED TO UNION:** January 6, 1912

OTHER INTERESTING FACTS:

1. Santa Fe, the capital of New Mexico, is located at the base of a range of mountains. This location is deceiving; Santa Fe is 7,000 feet above sea level, which means it is actually higher than the highest mountain east of the Mississippi. The entire state of New Mexico is a high state, with a dry climate. The eastern plains produce oil, wheat, and cattle. Forest-covered mountains, desert plateaus, and desert valleys predominate in the central and western areas.

2. New Mexico is the fifth-largest state, but its population is small and widely dispersed. Its ratio of water area to land area is smaller than that of any other state. The Rocky Mountains extend into its northern section. If you love to camp, fish, or ride a horse on wooded trails, these highlands are for you. A variety of large and small wildlife can still be found in these wild areas.

3. The Rio Grande runs out of Colorado and across New Mexico, then into Mexico. Human beings have lived in the Rio Grande valley for thousands of years. Here you will still find Pueblo Indians and Spanish-speaking Americans whose lives are similar to the lives of their long-ago ancestors.

SUPER FACT: *Did you know* that the first atomic bomb was exploded in the New Mexican desert in 1945?

NEW MEXICO

Unit•At•A•Glance

Read and complete all activities, beginning with **I** and ending with **V.**

I. Language

Use the words below
plus six of your own to
create a New Mexico
crossword or word-search puzzle.

    Rio Grande   roadrunner
    Santa Fe   piñon
    mountains   Rocky Mountains
    desert   atomic bomb

II. Environmental Studies

List three problems that might be caused
by the sparse population scattered over the
large land area in many parts of New
Mexico. Suggest a possible solution for
each of these problems.

III. Math

Design a time line to show the development of New Mexico from the time of the
first Spanish settlers in 1598 to the
development of the atomic bomb in 1945.

IV. Enrichment

Basket making is an art form that has provided vessels of rare beauty and
practical value for residents of New Mexico for thousands of years. New
Mexico's craft fairs, markets, and museums offer baskets representing
many different designs, materials, and ages.
Draw the design for a basket for a specific use
and list the materials needed.

V. Evaluation

Complete the "New Mexico Check-Up" worksheet.

NEW MEXICO

Check•Up

Plan a script for a TV documentary to be shot on location to tell the world about New Mexico. Include the geography, culture, major industries, scenic sites, natural resources, and state symbols plus other unique facts of interest to you.

OKLAHOMA

The Sooner State

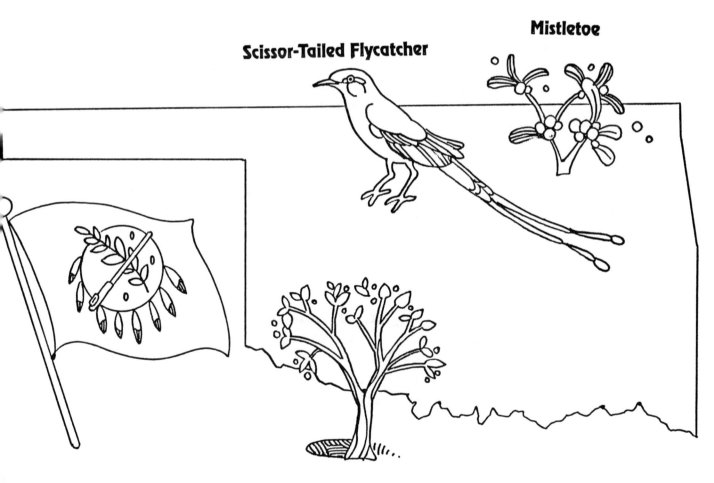

Scissor-Tailed Flycatcher

Mistletoe

Redbud

OKLAHOMA

Fact • Sheet

FAST FACTS

1. **CAPITAL:** Oklahoma City

2. **BORDERING STATES:** Texas, New Mexico, Colorado, Kansas, Arkansas, Missouri

3. **THREE MAJOR CITIES:** Oklahoma City • Tulsa • Lawton

4. **ADMITTED TO UNION:** November 16, 1907

OTHER INTERESTING FACTS:

1. Native Americans have played a major role in Oklahoma's history and development. They continue to contribute daily to the cultural, economic, and political welfare of this state. The name "Oklahoma" is derived from two Choctaw Indian words, "Okla," meaning "people," and "homma," meaning "red." More than 35 Indian tribes reside in Oklahoma today, making up one eighth of the nation's Native American population.

2. You could call Oklahoma home of the cowboys, too. Since the early days of cattle drives, when great herds of longhorn cattle were driven across famous Oklahoma trails (including, among many others, the old Chisholm Trail), to the present, with its modern-day ranches, cowboys have played an important role in Oklahoma's history.

3. In 1889, the first big land rush in Oklahoma Territory took place. Thousands of people from all over the country gathered for the signal: at noon, a soldier dropped a flag and blew a bugle. The land rush was on! Settlers rode horses and bicycles, and rode in wagons, and even a few locomotives, to hurry and grab their share of the land prize. Empty prairie land was filled with thousands of people by the end of the day. These sturdy people stayed to survive tornadoes and the hardships of living off the land.

SUPER FACT: *Did you know* that oil has been drilled in all but five of Oklahoma's seventy-seven counties? The Oklahoma state capital is the only capital in the world surrounded by producing oil wells.

Unit•At•A•Glance

Read and complete all activities, beginning with **I** and ending with **V**.

I. Language

In each list below mark out the word that does not belong:

Cherokee	cowboy	cattle	land
Choctaw	farmer	oil wells	homesteaders
Spanish	rodeo	refineries	panhandlers
Pawnee	herders	gold mines	settlers

II. Environmental Studies

Compare and contrast the life of a modern-day cowboy working in Oklahoma with today's conveniences and technology, to the life of an Oklahoma cowboy when the state was admitted to the Union in the early 1900's.

III. Math

Construct a time line to show the development of Oklahoma from homesteading in 1897 to present-day Oklahoma life.

IV. Enrichment

Imagine that you are the parent of a boy or girl your age who has just arrived with your family of four—a mother, father, older sister, and younger brother—to homestead in Oklahoma. There are no houses, schools, or even communities. Write a letter to a neighbor you left behind to tell about the geography, climate, your present housing, daily activities, challenges, and opportunities of your new life. Be sure to share your concerns for education for your children, concerns for economic security, loneliness for friends and relatives left behind, as well as your plans and dreams of a bright future. Remember, you believe in the opportunities offered by a new frontier, or you wouldn't have made the long and hard trip to Oklahoma.

V. Evaluation

Complete the "Oklahoma Check-Up" worksheet.

©1993 by Incentive Publications, Inc., Nashville, TN.

OKLAHOMA

Working from memory, make your own Oklahoma Fast Fact Sheet highlighting facts, features, and natural resources. Include as many specific details and points of interest as possible.

OKLAHOMA FAST FACTS

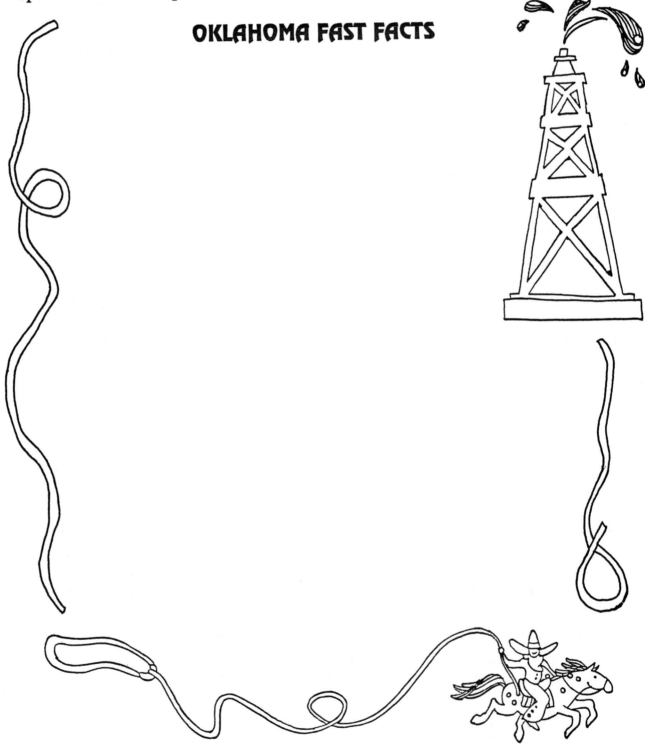

TEXAS

The Lone Star State

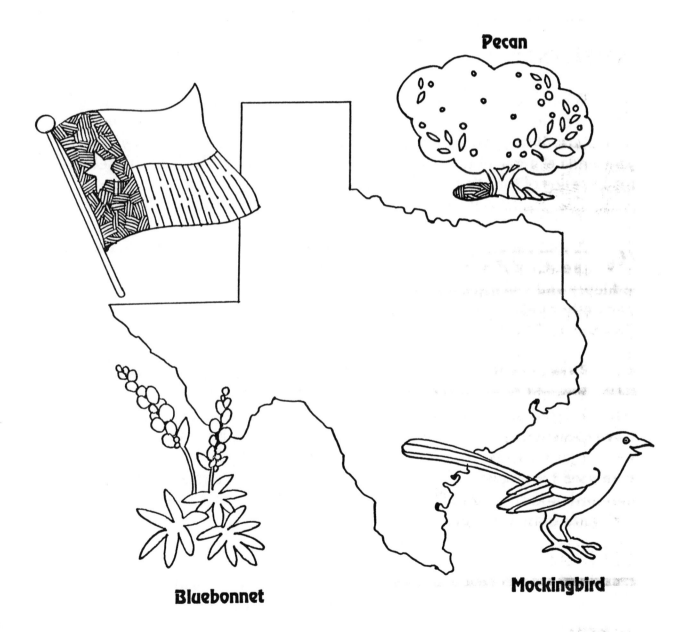

Pecan

Bluebonnet

Mockingbird

TEXAS

Fact • Sheet

—— FAST FACTS ——

1. **CAPITAL:** Austin

2. **BORDERING STATES:** New Mexico, Oklahoma, Arkansas, Louisiana

3. **THREE MAJOR CITIES:** Houston • Dallas • San Antonio

4. **ADMITTED TO UNION:** December 29, 1845

OTHER INTERESTING FACTS:

1. When big, sprawling Texas entered the Union, Congress suggested it divide into five states. But the choice was made to remain one large state. It has just about any kind of landscape you can think of: plains, thousands of acres of tangled growth in the east called the Big Thicket, the fertile valley of the Rio Grande, the Edwards Plateau with its sheep and goats, pine woods, rice-growing swamps, mountain country, and deserts.

2. A well called Spindletop, in Beaumont, Texas, is responsible for the growth of Houston as an oil center. In 1901 the well exploded suddenly and violently, and a copious flow of oil followed. There were to be many other gushing wells. Today, Texas oil is carried all over the world by pipelines and tankers.

3. Texas's cattle industry got its start when longhorn cattle were brought from Mexico by Spanish explorers. Herds of these cattle roamed Texas, sometimes mating with strays from wagon trains. Texans drove these herds to the railroad stations in Kansas, but the cattle were too lean for good eating. Ranchers worked on developing fatter animals that were good for producing beef. Some of these are the shorthorn, the Hereford, and the Santa Gertrudis. Texas produces more beef cattle, sheep, and goats than any other state.

SUPER FACT: *Did you know* that ranchers once provided "goat coats" for their Angoras after shearing them, to protect them from the weather?

Unit•At•A•Glance

Read and complete all activities, beginning with **I** and ending with **V**.

I. Language

Texas is a BIG state, second in size only to Alaska. List at least 22 words that describe or refer to Texas. Use your word list to design a word game to be played by a family driving across the state of Texas.

II. Environmental Studies

Imagine that you will be an exchange student in a Texas city for the next school year. You are free to choose from Dallas, Austin, or Houston. Name your city and list three reasons for your choice.

III. Math

Make up four word problems based on a school day in the Texas school of your choice. One should be based on purchasing school supplies, one on lunch, one on recreation, and one on an after-school activity. Solve your problems.

IV. Enrichment

Using the same city that you selected in Activity II, write a letter to the student with whom you will be exchanging places. Tell some of the ways you think life will be different in your school and how you would advise the boy or girl to be prepared to handle the differences. Ask questions so that you will be prepared to attend the new school.

V. Evaluation

Complete the "Texas Check-Up" worksheet.

TEXAS

Check•Up

Imagine that you have been employed to travel and promote Texas in order to encourage businesses and factories to relocate to the state. Design and make a brochure that includes information about the climate, natural resources, location, availability of labor, history, and living conditions. Use pictures and symbols to make your brochure more interesting. In the space below, list topics and/or make drawings that will be included in your brochure.

Western Mountain States

COLORADO

The Centennial State

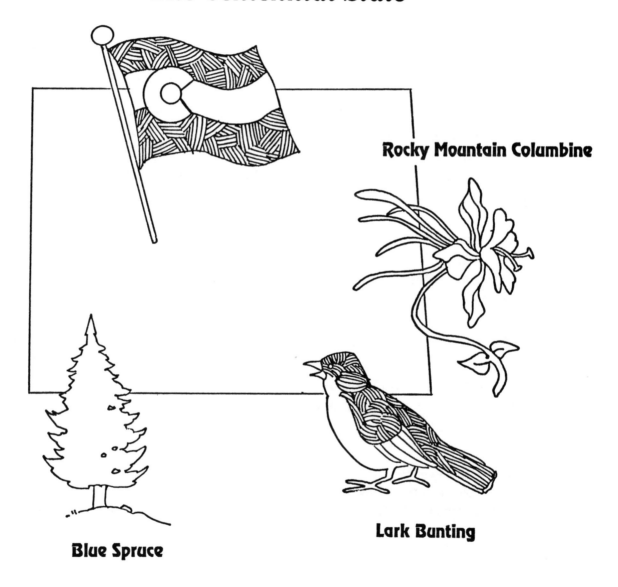

Rocky Mountain Columbine

Blue Spruce

Lark Bunting

COLORADO

Fact • Sheet

——— FAST FACTS ———

1. **CAPITAL:** Denver

2. **BORDERING STATES:** New Mexico, Utah, Wyoming, Nebraska, Kansas, Oklahoma

3. **THREE MAJOR CITIES:** Denver • Colorado Springs • Aurora

4. **ADMITTED TO UNION:** August 1, 1876

OTHER INTERESTING FACTS:

1. There are good reasons for Colorado's fame as "the state of mountains." With an average elevation of 6,800 feet, Colorado is the highest state in the U.S. Its many majestic mountains pay tribute to this state's rich history.

2. The discovery of gold and silver brought a heavy migration to the state in the mid- and late-1800's. Gold, silver, lead, zinc, and much of the world's molybdenum (a metal added to steel to make it especially strong) are mined in Colorado today.

3. Tourism contributes significantly to the state's present-day economy. Ski vacations are especially popular. Tourists spend millions of dollars each year in Colorado. Aspen has more ski lifts and trails than does any other ski resort in the nation.

SUPER FACT: *Did you know* that Colorado holds an important key to the world's food supply? Seeds from most food-bearing plants known to the American Department of Agriculture have been harvested and stored in concrete vaults in Fort Collins, Colorado. If any particular plant should become extinct, seeds from this treasure trove could be used to start new crops.

Unit•At•A•Glance

Read and complete all activities, beginning with **I** and ending with **V.**

I. Language

Imagine that you have been invited to enter a contest sponsored by the Colorado Department of Tourism. Contest entries will be judged on the basis of the quality of questions asked about the state and reasons given for wanting to visit Colorado as stated in a letter. The prize will be a one-week winter vacation in the Colorado Mountains. Write your letter!

II. Environmental Studies

Now imagine that you won the contest and you will be spending a week in Colorado. Think about the activities in which you will want to participate and the kind of weather you are apt to have. Plan your wardrobe for a week. Make a list of clothes you have and clothes you would need to buy.

III. Math

You have been given a budget of $550 to use for your one-week winter vacation. Your room in the lodge will cost $66 per day, but since you will be sharing the room with another winner, you will only be paying half of this amount per day. The cost of food per day will be $21. Recreation fees per day will add up to $15. Compute the cost per day and multiply it by seven to find out how much money you will have left to buy souvenirs.

IV. Enrichment

Make a list of the people for whom you would want to buy presents during your vacation. Decide what you would like to buy for each person, how much you would spend for each gift, and how much you would want to save for a special souvenir of your own. Draw a picture of your own souvenir.

V. Evaluation

Complete the "Colorado Check-Up" worksheet.

COLORADO

Check • Up

Find the words in the puzzle to fill in the blanks in the sentences below.
You will find the words across, up, and down.

R	S	D	O	U	L	G	N	R	T	M	Z
O	G	C	D	R	N	S	O	V	M	O	N
C	O	L	U	M	B	I	N	E	D	L	A
K	L	A	R	K	U	L	E	B	E	Y	C
Y	D	Z	D	E	N	V	B	F	N	B	G
M	H	I	J	K	T	E	R	L	V	D	M
O	D	N	P	Q	I	R	A	S	E	E	T
U	N	C	U	V	N	W	S	X	R	N	Y
N	Z	A	B	C	G	D	K	E	F	U	G
T	O	U	R	I	S	M	A	H	I	M	K
A	S	P	E	N	L	M	N	O	P	Q	R
I	T	S	U	V	W	X	Y	Z	A	B	C
N	F	O	R	T	C	O	L	L	I	N	S

1. The _____ _____ _____
   is the Colorado state flower.
2. The capital of Colorado is _____.
3. The name of one of the states bordering Colorado is _____.
4. Tons of _____ and _____ lured settlers to Colorado
   in the 1800's.
5. _____ is now the main attraction in Colorado.
6. _____ has more ski lifts and trails than any other ski resort
   in the nation.
7. The _____ _____ is the Colorado state bird.
8. _____ is a metal added to steel to make it super strong.
9. Another of the metals now mined in Colorado, other than gold and
   silver, is _____.
10. A seed from nearly every food plant we know is preserved in concrete
    vaults in _____ _____, Colorado.

IDAHO

The Gem State

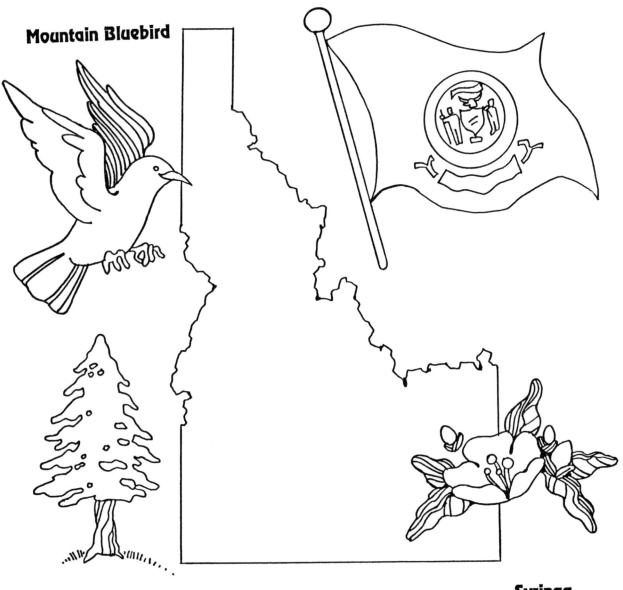

Mountain Bluebird

Western White Pine

Syringa

IDAHO

Fact • Sheet

FAST FACTS

1. **CAPITAL:** Boise

2. **BORDERING STATES:** Washington, Oregon, Nevada, Utah, Wyoming, Montana

3. **THREE MAJOR CITIES:** Boise • Pocatello • Idaho Falls

4. **ADMITTED TO UNION:** July 3, 1890

OTHER INTERESTING FACTS:

1. Everyone associates the production of potatoes with Idaho. Idaho is the biggest producer of potatoes in the United States! But potatoes are not its only crop. Other significant crops are barley, sugar beets, hay, beans, peas, hops, mint, onions, and fruit (Idaho produces the most American barley). Livestock production is also important in Idaho.

2. Idaho was the 43rd state admitted to the Union. The state capitol building in Boise took fifteen years to build—it was finished in 1920. Its interior is a fabulous blend of different types of marble: green marble from Vermont, gray marble from Alaska, reddish-pink marble from Georgia, and black marble from Italy.

3. Idaho's vast acreage of forest land is used by many commercial, environmental, and scientific groups. Often these groups are in conflict with one another over the use of this land. The National Park System oversees the 21 million acres of forest, and tries to balance the claims of mining, logging, and vacation interests, and the claims of those who are interested in scientific research and protecting our national resources.

SUPER FACT: *Did you know* that a painting by a woman named Emma Edwards Green was designed to be used as the Great Seal of Idaho? No other state in the nation has a great seal designed by a woman.

Unit•At•A•Glance

Read and complete all activities, beginning with **I** and ending with **V.**

I. Language

It is brown and knobby, is grown a
lot in Idaho, and never sees the light
of day until it is ready to be fried,
boiled, or baked. What is it?
Solve this riddle and write three
more of your own about Idaho. Ask a friend to solve your riddles.

II. Environmental Studies

Create a travel brochure for Idaho. Include important cities, national
parks, historical and cultural sites, natural wonders, and tourist
attractions. Illustrate your brochure with as much detail as possible.

III. Math

Plan a visit to the three largest cities in Idaho.
List the cities and use the state map to
determine the distance from one city to
another. List these distances, then add them
together to
find the total
number of
miles to be
traveled. Beside each figure, list the
distance in metric terms.

IV. Enrichment

Draw, label, and cut out figures
representative of Idaho. Use a wire clothes
hanger, string, and tape to make a mobile
to hang in honor of the state.

V. Evaluation

Complete the "Idaho Check-Up" worksheet.

IDAHO

Check•Up

Unscramble the words in the scrambled-word list and use them to complete the sentences below to show how much you know about Idaho.

AHDOI SLAFL	TANNOUMI BERDULBI
STATPEOO	TMNREVO
RSGAYIN	MGE
TYLAI	SHAWGTNINO
GRIAOGE	HUAT
YLERAB	GOLNIGG
KSLAAA	GNIMNI

1. The marble inside the Idaho state capitol building in Boise comes from
   _____, _____, _____, and _____.

2. Idaho is the chief producer of _____ and _____ in the
   United States.

3. Idaho is also known as the _____ state.

4. The _____ is the state flower of Idaho.

5. Three major cities of Idaho are Boise, Pocatello, and _____
   _____.

6. Two the the six states that border Idaho are _____ and
   _____.

7. Two industries that affect the ecology of Idaho are _____ and
   _____.

8. The state bird of Idaho is the _____ _____.

MONTANA

The Treasure State

Western Meadow Lark

Bitterroot

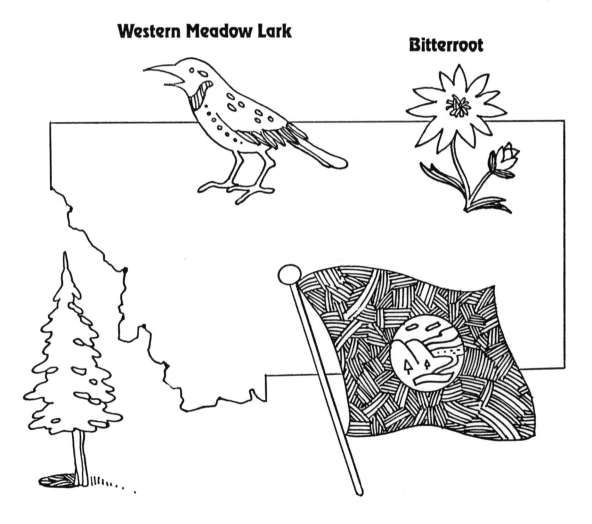

Ponderosa Pine

MONTANA

Fact • Sheet

> ─── **FAST FACTS** ───
>
> 1. **CAPITAL:** Helena
>
> 2. **BORDERING STATES:** Idaho, Wyoming, North Dakota, South Dakota
>
> 3. **THREE MAJOR CITIES:** Billings • Great Falls • Missoula
>
> 4. **ADMITTED TO UNION:** November 8, 1889

OTHER INTERESTING FACTS:

1. Montana is the fourth-largest state in the Union, but it is a relatively empty state, with few large cities and towns. Many Montana ranchers are accustomed to driving for an hour or more to buy food or to attend a social event. The Montana life for children who don't live in a town might mean getting an education in a one-room schoolhouse, and learning to ride a horse or drive a tractor at an age when most children have not even learned to ride a bicycle.

2. Big Montana includes many different kinds of land. In the west are the Rocky Mountains. In Glacier National Park, there are streams flowing through a place called Triple Divide Pass, some of which eventually flow into the Atlantic Ocean, some into the Pacific, and some into Hudson Bay. In this Big Sky country, you can sometimes build a snowman in August! East of the mountains are rolling plains that are home to sheep and cattle. Farther east are wheat fields and underground deposits of natural gas, oil, and coal.

3. Early settlers first rushed into Montana with the discovery of gold and silver, but now other minerals are more important to the state. Butte, Montana, is located atop one of the world's largest copper deposits. Some fear that the open copper mine may someday grow so large that the town of Butte will disappear into it!

SUPER FACT: *Did you know* that Charles Russell, a Montana cowboy, grew famous around the world for his paintings of the Old West? One of his most famous paintings is a painting of the Lewis and Clark meeting with the Indians in Bitter Root Valley.

Unit•At•A•Glance

Read and complete all activities, beginning with **I** and ending with **V.**

I. Language

Draw two large, overlapping circles. Try to fill one circle with nouns that name persons, places, or things found in Montana. Then in the other circle write adjectives that could be used to describe the state. Match nouns and adjectives to find descriptive items. Fill the overlapping circle with these descriptive phrases.

II. Environmental Studies

Pretend that you are moving to a Montana ranch to open up a new business. Describe the kind of business you would open and give reasons to support your choice.

III. Math

Draw a dot-to-dot picture of a Montana mountain goat or grizzly bear, using odd numbers only from 3 to 53. Ask a friend to follow the dots to complete the picture.

IV. Enrichment

Draw, color, and cut out pictures of the descriptive phrases from the overlapping circle in the language activity to use for a Montana collage. Arrange the pictures on a sheet of drawing paper and paste in place. Add background scenery and/or additional drawings to complete the collage.

V. Evaluation

Complete the "Montana Check-Up" worksheet.

MONTANA

Draw or paint a picture, or make a collage, including at least ten signs, symbols, phrases, or pictures that have something to do with Montana. Ask a friend to play a Montana memory game with you. Ask the friend to study your portrayal of the state for one minute. Then completely cover the picture and have the friend name as many of the items as possible. It would be fun to follow up by asking the friend to test your memory with a list of words instead of pictures.

NEVADA

The Silver State

Mountain Bluebird

Single-leaf Piñon

Sagebrush

NEVADA

Fact • Sheet

```
┌─────────────────────────────── FAST FACTS ───┐
│                                               │
│  1. CAPITAL: Carson City                      │
│                                               │
│  2. BORDERING STATES: California, Arizona, Utah, Idaho, Oregon │
│                                               │
│  3. THREE MAJOR CITIES: Las Vegas • Reno • Paradise │
│                                               │
│  4. ADMITTED TO UNION: October 31, 1864       │
│                                               │
└───────────────────────────────────────────────┘
```

OTHER INTERESTING FACTS:

1. Most of Nevada is rugged country, with mysterious, forbidding mountain ranges. There is a scarcity of drinking water, few paved highways—and lots of dust! The reason for the lack of water is simple: there is very little rainfall. Nevada is called the "driest state."

2. Tourists sometimes travel to Nevada in order to experience its cool high deserts and perhaps to feel a bit of a thrill by visiting some of its ghost towns. These visits are short, however, and the greatest amount of money coming into Nevada comes through the gambling casinos in Reno and Las Vegas.

3. Nevada's salt flats and shallow lake beds yield a rich harvest of fossilized bones of prehistoric animals. You may have an image of bones of modern domestic and wild animals lying in the desert when you think of Nevada. A famous American artist, Georgia O'Keeffe, used these bones as images in many of her paintings.

SUPER FACT: *Did you know* that forty percent of all the towns in Nevada are ghost towns? These are towns that were built because of gold- and silver-mining prospects, and were deserted when the precious metals ran out.

NEVADA

Unit•At•A•Glance

Read and complete all activities, beginning with **I** and ending with **V.**

I. Language

A famous old saying is, "First impressions are lasting." Write a newspaper feature story telling what you think a visitor's first impression of Nevada would be.

II. Environmental Studies

Imagine that you have been given the power to give a gift of one million dollars to the people of Nevada. The only catch is that the money must go for something that will help to make the life of today's children more environmentally safe. Write a proposal for what you will spend the money for and your plan for doing it.

III. Math

Nevada was the 36th state to be admitted to the Union. Write 1864 in Roman numerals. Now write the present year in Roman numerals. Subtract to find out how many years Nevada has been a member of the United States. Write your answer in Roman numerals.

IV. Enrichment

Fifty years ago many of the jobs in Nevada were considered to be jobs for men only. Fold a sheet of drawing paper vertically into three parts. Select three jobs that have traditionally been held by men. With crayons or markers, show a woman doing one of these jobs today in each panel. List the skills needed for each job underneath the picture.

V. Evaluation

Complete the "Nevada Check-Up" worksheet.

© 1993 by Incentive Publications, Inc., Nashville, TN.

NEVADA

Complete the banners below to be used to acquaint a prospective visitor with information about Nevada.

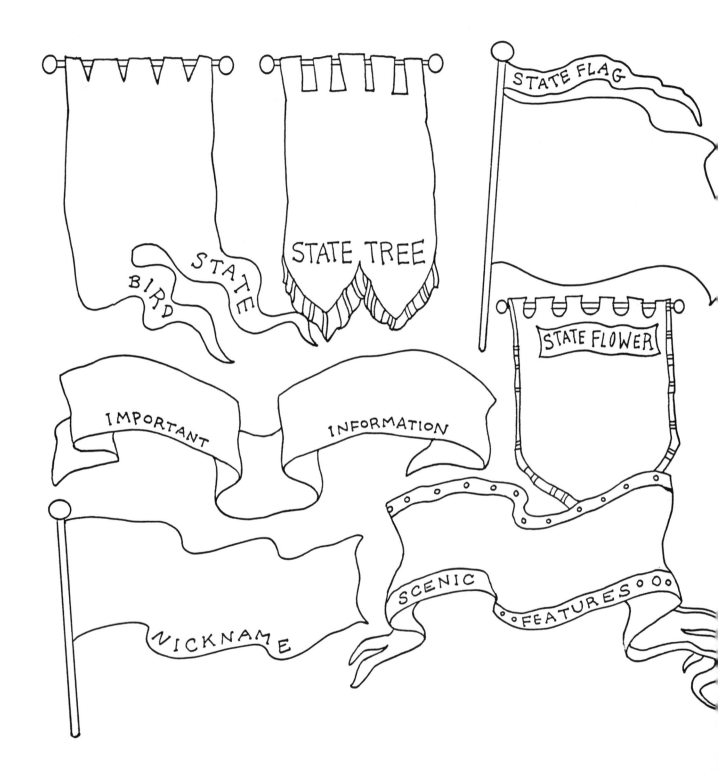

UTAH

The Beehive State

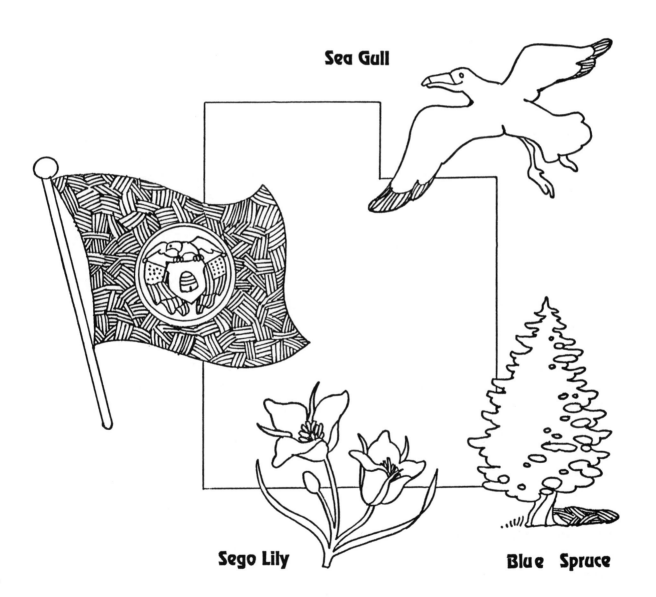

Sea Gull

Sego Lily

Blue Spruce

UTAH

Fact • Sheet

FAST FACTS

1. **CAPITAL:** Salt Lake City

2. **BORDERING STATES:** Colorado, Wyoming, Idaho, Nevada, Arizona

3. **THREE MAJOR CITIES:** Salt Lake City • West Valley City • Provo

4. **ADMITTED TO UNION:** January 4, 1896

OTHER INTERESTING FACTS:

1. The Great Salt Lake in Utah is the largest lake west of the Mississippi. It is salty because it receives water from many streams, but there is no outlet through which the water can leave; thus mineral salts that are carried into the lake remain. It is eight times more salty than the ocean. The only form of life that can survive in the Salt Lake is a tiny shrimp that is used in making fish food. Nearby Salt Lake City was founded by the Mormon leader Brigham Young, who arrived in the Salt Lake Valley in 1847 with a party of hard-working, resourceful pioneers.

2. The magnificent mountains of Utah attract a steady stream of hikers, campers, skiers, and sightseers. The mountains also provide pastures for livestock and supply copper, gold, lead, and zinc.

3. Even though the nearest ocean is more than five hundred miles away, the sea gull was named the official bird of Utah. In 1847, early Mormon settlers were dismayed by hordes of crickets that arrived to destroy their newly planted crops. Mysterious flocks of sea gulls flew over to Salt Lake City from Great Salt Lake to eat up swarms of the crop-devouring crickets.

SUPER FACT: *Did you know* that Utah is the home of five national parks? They are (1) Zion, (2) Bryce Canyon, (3) Canyonlands, (4) Arches, and (5) Capitol Reef.

Unit•At•A•Glance

Read and complete all activities, beginning with **I** and ending with **V.**

I. Language

Select one of Utah's national parks to use as
the subject for a videotape script. Try to
highlight the scenic and recreational
attractions, the plant and animal wildlife,
and the features of interest. Provide captions
for your script and illustrate each feature.

II. Environmental Studies

Write ten clues about Utah. Ask a friend to
use the clues to identify the state. Turnabout is fair play. Ask your friend to
write ten clues for you to use to identify another state.

III. Math

Utah was admitted to the Union in 1896.
Subtract to find out how many years this
state has been a member of the Union.
Delaware was the first state admitted to
the Union in 1787. Subtract to find out how
much longer Delaware has been a state
than Utah. Use these two dates to write
two word problems. Solve the problems.

IV. Enrichment

Design a "Remember the Seagull" press kit to
honor the famous bird that saved Utah's crops
from crickets in 1847. Include a bumper sticker,
a poster, and a newspaper feature article in your
kit. Add any other items that you think will help
people remember this important event.

V. Evaluation

Complete the "Utah Check-Up" worksheet.

UTAH

Check•Up

Write down the first twelve things that come to mind when you think about Utah. Read over the list and think carefully about each statement. Write *fact* beside the statements you can actually prove from your study of the state and *opinion* beside the statements that you think may be true. Count up your number of facts and your number of opinions to check your "factual knowledge" of Utah. Later, find out how many of your opinions were factual.

1. _____ _____

_____

2. _____ _____

_____

3. _____ _____

_____

4. _____ _____

_____

5. _____ _____

_____

6. _____ _____

_____

7. _____ _____

_____

8. _____ _____

_____

9. _____ _____

_____

10. _____ _____

_____

WYOMING

The Equality State

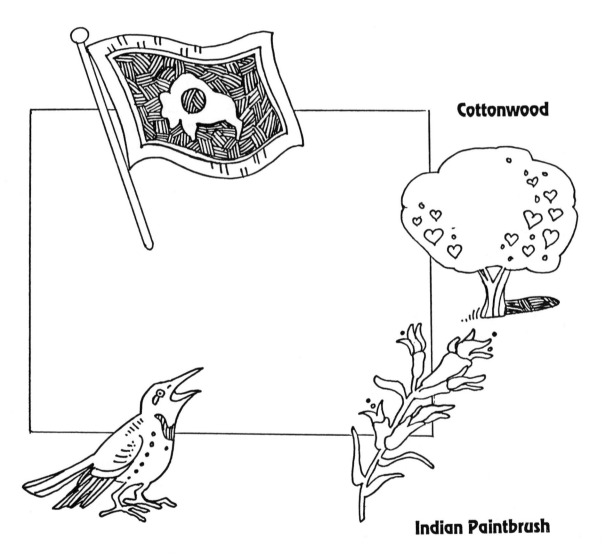

Cottonwood

Indian Paintbrush

Meadow Lark

WYOMING

Fact • Sheet

FAST FACTS

1. **CAPITAL:** Cheyenne

2. **BORDERING STATES:** Colorado, Utah, Idaho, Montana, South Dakota, Nebraska

3. **THREE MAJOR CITIES:** Cheyenne • Casper • Laramie

4. **ADMITTED TO UNION:** July 10, 1890

OTHER INTERESTING FACTS:

1. ❑ Wyoming, "The Equality State," was the first state (then a territory) to grant women the right to vote and the right to hold office, in 1869. The truth is that women were scarce in Wyoming, and the men hoped to attract women to the territory by giving them the right to vote! The first woman governor in the nation, Nellie Taylor Ross, served in Wyoming in 1924.

2. ❑ Wyoming has fewer people per square mile than does any other state except Alaska. It is a wild region, with a dry and windy climate and high mountains. It has more than 600 species of free-roaming wildlife, including many that have disappeared from other states. You can still find herds of antelope and wild horses in Wyoming, as well as golden eagles, grizzly bears, elk, bighorn sheep, bald eagles, and great blue herons.

3. ❑ The geothermal wonders of Yellowstone National Park had their beginnings in an enormous volcanic eruption 600,000 years ago. A huge reservoir of melted rock still exists beneath the surface, and provides the heat that causes Yellowstone's famous hot water and steam events such as geysers, hot springs, and hissing steam vents. Visitors are also amazed by the 27 petrified forests, once-living forests that were buried and preserved by volcanic ash.

SUPER FACT: *Did you know* that oil, of which Wyoming is the sixth-largest producer in the nation, was once mixed with flour by pioneers and used to grease the squeaking wheels of their covered wagons?

WYOMING

Unit•At•A•Glance

Read and complete all activities, beginning with **I** and ending with **V**.

I. Language

Design a picture postcard with a scene representing Yellowstone National Park. Pretend you are visiting the park for the first time. Address the card to a friend. Then write a message to your friend telling about the highlights of your visit.

II. Environmental Studies

Design two complete outfits, including shoes and hats, for someone your age living in Wyoming. One should be for winter wear and one for summer wear.

III. Math

Tell why each of the following measurement devices would be important to Wyoming's sheep growers. Then write a word problem using the stated measurements.

Clock:	hours, minutes
Calendar:	months, weeks
Scale:	pounds, ounces

IV. Enrichment

Design a poster to warn visitors to Yellowstone not to feed the grizzly bears that still roam the park. Be sure to use a picture of the grizzly, who looks quite harmless but who can be very dangerous.

V. Evaluation

Complete the "Wyoming Check-Up" worksheet.

WYOMING

Check•Up

Write a feature article for the Sunday newspaper based on the state of Wyoming. Include as much factual information and folklore in the article as possible. Be sure to name the state symbols, capital, bordering states, and natural resources. Give your article a headline and yourself a byline.

Pacific Coast States

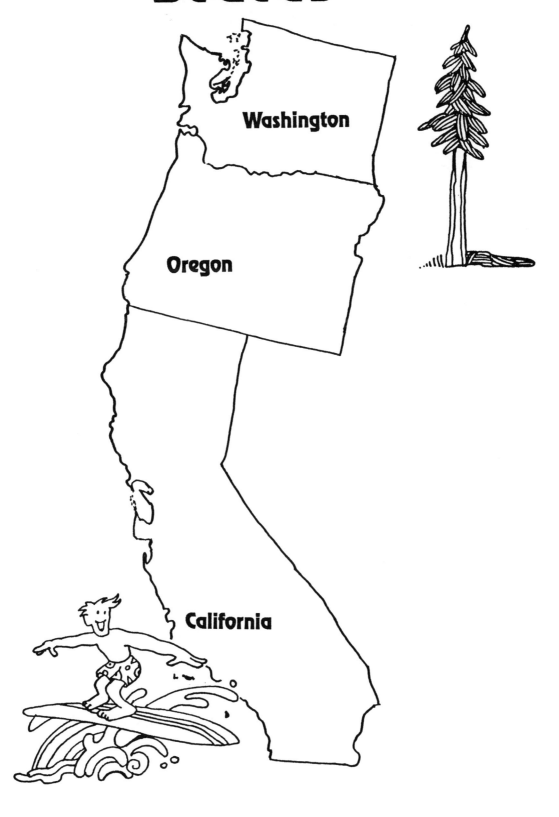

Washington

Oregon

California

CALIFORNIA

The Golden State

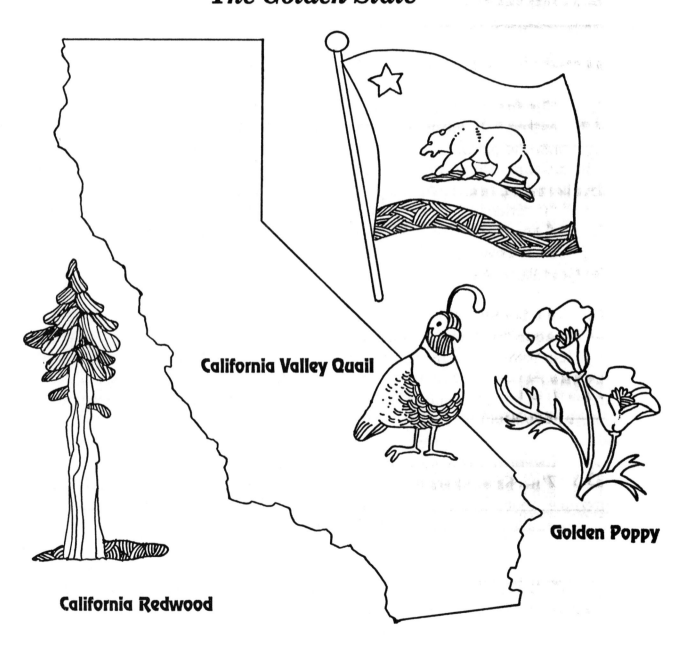

California Valley Quail

California Redwood

Golden Poppy

CALIFORNIA

Fact • Sheet

━ FAST FACTS ━

1. **CAPITAL:** Sacramento

2. **BORDERING STATES:** Oregon, Nevada, Arizona

3. **THREE MAJOR CITIES:** Los Angeles • San Diego • San José

4. **ADMITTED TO UNION:** September 9, 1850

OTHER INTERESTING FACTS:

1. The first Californians were Native Americans who lived off the land, eating fish, animals, acorns, and wild plants. In 1769, Spanish explorers and priests arrived and, with the help of the Native Americans, built missions along the coastline. San Francisco, a fascinating city whose streets run up and down steep hills that stand above a fog-filled harbor, is one of the cities in California that began as a mission. The city's destiny changed one day in 1848, when a man rushed into town shouting that gold had been discovered in the American River. The news spread like fire, and the Gold Rush was on.

2. As do many of the western states, California has water problems. Aqueducts, pipes, and ditches carry the water of mountain rivers, that has been stored in reservoirs, to California farms and cities. The Los Angeles Aqueduct carries water from the Owens River, a distance of 223 miles. It is hard to believe that before these irrigation systems were built, many of California's lush farms were desert.

3. California is a state of diversity, in climate, crops, and ways of life. The climate ranges from cold and snowy to subtropical. California produces more food than any other state. In fact, there are few countries that produce more food than California!

SUPER FACT: *Did you know* that California has more people and more cars than does any other state?

Unit•At•A•Glance

Read and complete all activities, beginning with **I** and ending with **V**.

I. Language

California is a large and diverse state, offering various climates, types of geography, cultures, and occupational opportunities. Based on what you have learned about the state, select the place in the state that you would most like to live. Write a letter to the editor of the local newspaper giving reasons for your choice.

II. Environmental Studies

Because Californians have access to an abundance of fresh fruit and

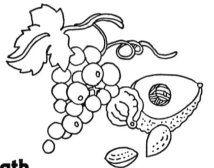

vegetables along with an interest in good health practices, many are vegetarians, committed to eating no animal products. Write out a five-day balanced menu plan, using only fruits, vegetables, and nuts, for a person living in California.

III. Math

Most tourists believe that California does live up to its nickname, "The Golden State." Survey four people to find out the reason they would most like to visit California and the city they would most like to visit. Graph your findings.

IV. Enrichment

Design a gift, appropriate for a person your age, to be made from natural resources of California. Examples: shells from the seashore, redwood bark, grasses, seed pods or nuts, etc. Describe the gift and design a gift card with a message to the person you would send it to.

V. Evaluation

Complete the "California Check-Up" worksheet.

CALIFORNIA

Check • Up

Create a "California Grab Bag" game to play with a friend.
Use crayons or markers to decorate a medium-sized brown
paper bag to represent California. On strips of paper or
index cards, write or draw words, phrases, signs, symbols,
and scenes to represent the state. For a good game you
will need a minimum of 24 cards. Number each card
(1-24) and write the number in the corner. On a separate
piece of paper, list the answers in order corresponding
to each page number. Place the cards in the bag
and ask a friend to play the game with you.
Players take turns drawing a card from the bag
and telling how it relates to the state. When a card is properly identified, it
is added to that player's stack of cards. When the bag is empty, the player
with the most cards becomes the winner. Write or draw the information for
your playing cards in the space below.

OREGON

The Beaver State

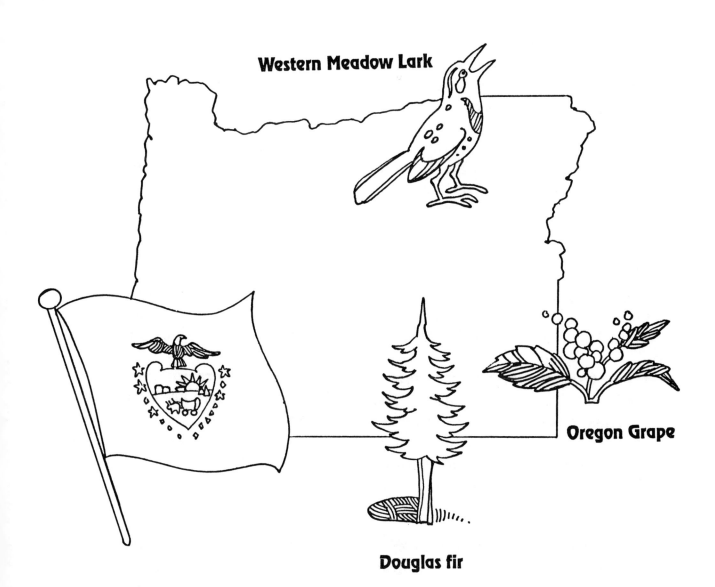

Western Meadow Lark

Oregon Grape

Douglas fir

OREGON

Fact • Sheet

FAST FACTS

1. **CAPITAL:** Salem

2. **BORDERING STATES:** California, Nevada, Idaho, Washington

3. **THREE MAJOR CITIES:** Portland • Eugene • Salem

4. **ADMITTED TO UNION:** February 14, 1859

OTHER INTERESTING FACTS:

1. Oregon is first among American states in the production of lumber and wood products. Some of the types of forest trees that cover 50 percent of the state are Douglas fir, hemlock, and Ponderosa pine. Coos Bay and Portland are ports from which much of the lumber is shipped— most of it to Japan! U.S. inland consumers of this lumber receive their shipments by trucks and trains. Every part of a tree, from the bark to the sawdust that appears when lumber is cut, can be used in some way. Some of the products made from what might seem to be "waste" are plywood, chipboard, paper, and garden mulch.

2. Most of the population of Oregon resides in cities and towns in the valley of the Willamette River: Portland, Salem (the capital of Oregon), Albany, and Eugene. Salem is noted for its canning and freezing factories, Albany is the home of refineries that treat scarce metals for use in nuclear reactors, and Eugene is surrounded by wood-products factories.

3. Oregon's coast might seem like a paradise to hikers and cyclers looking for challenging trails along the shore. There are also sandy beaches that will give up their clams to those willing to dig, and places you can swim among gulls and sea lions. Near Bandon you can see "sea stacks," islands of rock in eerie shapes that have been formed by the battle between the ocean and the land.

SUPER FACT: *Did you know* that a salmon travels back to spawn in the brook of its birth by swimming hundreds of miles upstream, even jumping over waterfalls? It uses its sense of smell to find the correct stream! The two major types of salmon are Chinook and Pacific salmon.

Unit•At•A•Glance

Read and complete all activities, beginning with **I** and ending with **V.**

I. Language

Probably no other coastline in the world surpasses Oregon's rugged coastal trail. Picture in your mind the hills, rocks, inlets, caves, and crashing sea. Write a poem, a song, or a myth about this majestic scene.

II. Environmental Studies

Preserving the tall trees and forests of Oregon is of great concern to conservation-conscious citizens. Design a poster or full-page magazine ad to encourage wise use of our nation's diminishing natural resources.

III. Math

Make a list of ten math terms that would be important to loggers and lumber workers.

IV. Enrichment

Use only three colors to draw or paint an illustration for your original poem, song, or myth. Choose your colors carefully to reflect the work's mood.

V. Evaluation

Complete the "Oregon Check-Up" worksheet.

OREGON

Find the words in the puzzle to fill in the blanks in the sentences below. You will find the words across, up, and down.

W	V	P	O	R	T	L	A	N	D	A	B	C
I	A	S	P	A	W	N	B	C	S	S	R	H
L	L	E	F	G	H	I	J	K	E	T	O	I
L	L	M	N	O	P	Q	R	S	A	A	O	N
A	E	U	G	E	N	E	U	W	A	C	K	O
M	Y	X	Y	Z	A	B	C	D	S	K	S	O
E	F	P	I	C	N	I	C	G	H	S	J	K
T	K	L	M	N	O	P	Q	R	S	T	F	U
T	E	N	M	I	L	L	I	O	W	V	I	W
E	S	A	L	E	M	Y	Y	Z	I	B	S	C
B	I	K	E	D	E	F	G	H	M	J	H	K
C	L	A	M	S	L	M	N	O	P	Q	R	S
P	A	C	I	F	I	C	T	H	I	K	E	U

1. The three major cities in Oregon are

   _____, _____,

   and _____.

2. Most of Oregon's people live and work in
   Portland and smaller cities and towns
   in the _____ _____.

3. The _____ and _____ salmon leap waterfalls and swim
   hundreds of miles upstream to _____ in the _____
   where they were born.

4. Oregon's coastline offers a variety of scenery and activities. You can dig
   for _____ on sandy beaches or _____ in the surf.

5. Unusual islands of rock near Bandon are called _____ _____.

WASHINGTON

The Evergreen State

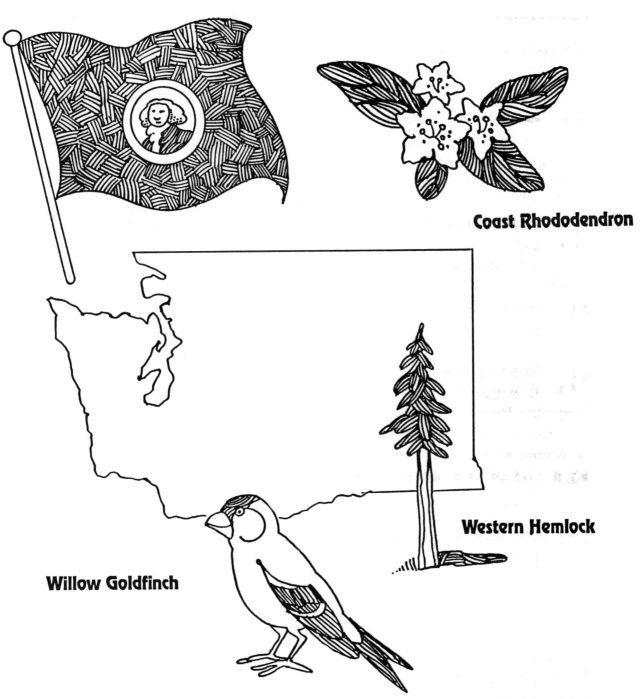

Coast Rhododendron

Western Hemlock

Willow Goldfinch

WASHINGTON

Fact • Sheet

---- **FAST FACTS** ----

1. **CAPITAL:** Olympia

2. **BORDERING STATES:** Oregon, Idaho

3. **THREE MAJOR CITIES:** Seattle • Spokane • Tacoma

4. **ADMITTED TO UNION:** November 11, 1889

OTHER INTERESTING FACTS:

1. The west coast of Washington has one of the heaviest yearly rainfalls in the nation. Over 200 inches a year fall on Mount Olympus, while western river valleys average 140 inches of rain a year. Olympia and other Puget Sound cities do not receive as much rainfall because they are protected from the elements by mountains.

2. Puget Sound is a body of seawater that, on a map, looks as if it were carved into the land. The Sound is what makes it possible for ships to travel from Seattle out into the Pacific, to Asia and Alaska. The shipping industry received a boost when the Alaska oil pipeline was being built, for there was a demand for supplies to be shipped to Alaska. Today Alaskan oil is carried into Puget Sound on tankers.

3. The Cascade Mountains split the state into two terrains, damp forestland in the west, and dry plateau in the east. The great Columbia River forges through the east, winding up as part of the border between Washington and Oregon. The Grand Coulee Dam is one of many Columbia River dams that brought "farm-ability" to the eastern desert, in which now grow potatoes, sugar beets, fruits, and other crops.

SUPER FACT: *Did you know* that Washington produces more aluminum than does any other state in the Union? It is made in Spokane, Vancouver, Longview, and other cities.

Unit•At•A•Glance

Read and complete all activities, beginning with **I** and ending with **V**.

I. Language

Washington's heavy rainfall contributes significantly to the state's economy and lifestyles. Create a series of three rainy-day pictures, not necessarily in sequence. They may even depict different times or have different characters or elements. The one required similarity is that all of them show a Washington setting. Order the pictures to provide a plot for an original story, select one of the following titles, and write an original story based on your pictures.

• Rain, rain, go away, we want to play.
• It rained for forty days and forty nights.
• Another day without sunshine will be one rainy day too many.

II. Environmental Studies

Even though the grand man-made dams of Washington have contributed greatly to the state's economic security, their construction and maintenance have caused displacement and upheaval to the habitats of people, animals, and plants. Compare and contrast the gains and losses to citizens living in the vicinity of the dams before and after their construction.

III. Math

Create a complex math story-problem based on apple-growing in Washington. Include a bushel, a peck, and a pound, and require the use of more than one math process. Write out the problem and ask a friend to solve it. Check the answer.

IV. Enrichment

Expand on your math story-problem to make it into an adventure story. Illustrate your story with a series of drawings, a collage, or a mural.

V. Evaluation

Complete the "Washington Check-Up" worksheet.

WASHINGTON

Check•Up

On the back of this page, list twenty words that
describe or relate to the state of Washington.
Think hard about each of the words you listed.
Then cross out ten, leaving only the ten that
describe the state in the most specific way.
Write each of the twenty words on half of one of
the puzzle strips below. On the other half of the
strip draw a picture to illustrate the word. Cut
the strips apart and place word strips in one
stack and picture strips in another. Put a rubber band around each set of
strips to hold them together. Test a friend's knowledge of Washington by
asking your friend to match the words and pictures and to tell how each
relates to the state.

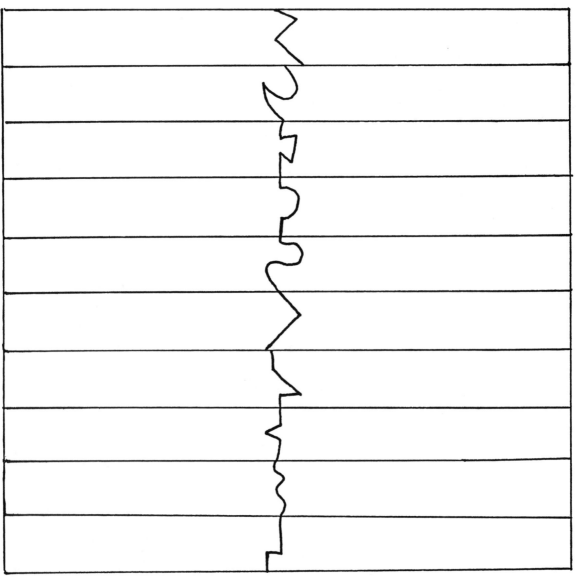

Alaska and Hawaii

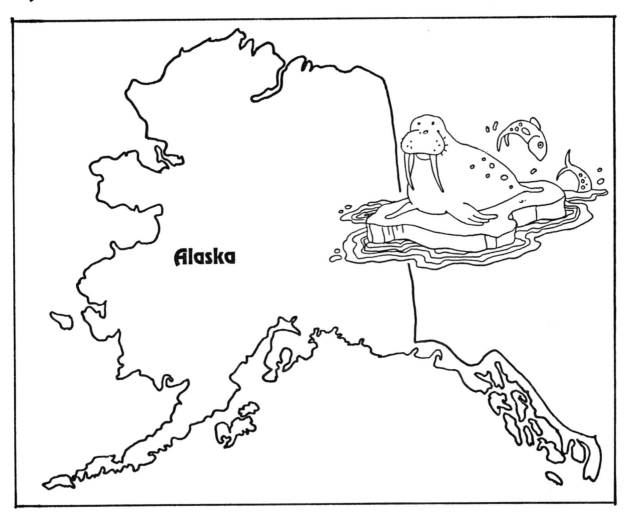

Alaska

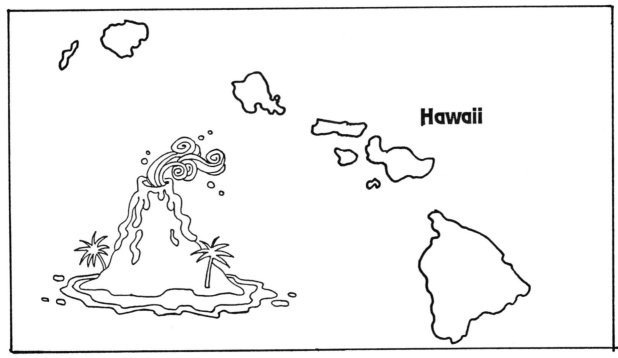

Hawaii

ALASKA

The Last Frontier

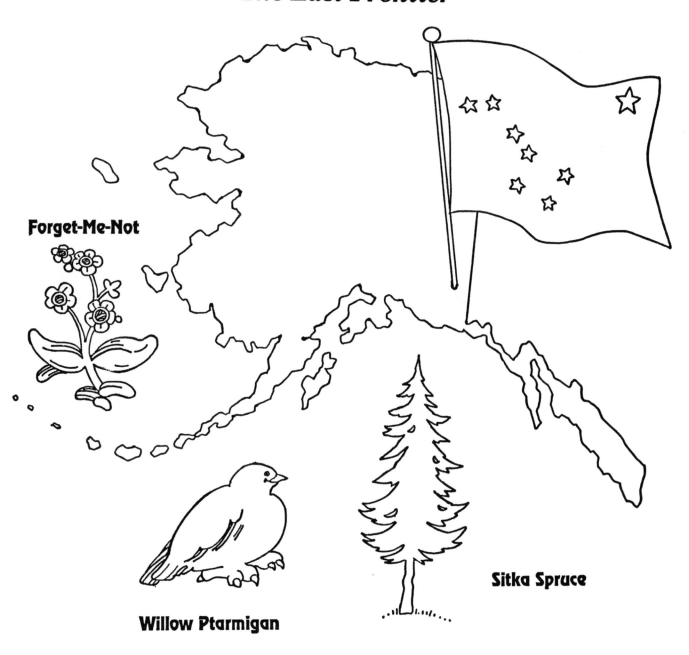

Forget-Me-Not

Willow Ptarmigan

Sitka Spruce

ALASKA

Fact • Sheet

FAST FACTS

1. **CAPITAL:** Juneau

2. **BORDERING STATES:** None

3. **THREE MAJOR CITIES:** Anchorage • Fairbanks • Juneau

4. **ADMITTED TO UNION:** January 3, 1959

OTHER INTERESTING FACTS:

1. Because of its rugged beauty and abundant wildlife, Alaska is a favorite destination for many tourists. Bus touring companies, cruise ships, and airlines compete for the tourist trade by trying to develop new and more exciting tour packages each year.

2. Although it was the next-to-the-last state to be admitted to the Union, Alaska boasts many "firsts." Alaska is the largest state in the Union and is more than twice the size of Texas, which is the next largest. Mount McKinley (located in Alaska) is the highest mountain peak in North America. Alaska is also first in commercial fishing in the United States, and the walrus is found only in this state.

3. Native Alaskans, whose ancestors lived in Alaska thousands of years ago, include the Eskimos, Aleuts, and Indians. In a historic congressional act, these native groups were granted ownership of large portions of Alaska where they also control rights to the natural resources, including oil. As are fishing, logging, and hunting, the oil industry is very important to Alaska. Agriculture is not an important industry, because Alaska has a very short growing season.

SUPER FACT: *Did you know* that the Alaskan brown bear is the largest meat-eating land animal in the world?

Unit•At•A•Glance

Read and complete all activities, beginning with **I** and ending with **V**.

I. Language

Pretend that you are a tourist visiting Alaska. Write a letter to a friend describing the scenery, wildlife, people, and other highlights of your visit. Use lots of descriptive words to make your letter interesting.

II. Environmental Studies

Weigh the advantages and disadvantages of fishing, hunting, and lumbering as occupations in Alaska today. Choose the one you find most interesting and write a job description for it.

III. Math

Interview ten friends to find out what Alaskan animal each would most like to see in its natural habitat. Graph your findings.

IV. Enrichment

Salmon, crab, halibut, shrimp, and herring are some of Alaska's most "fished-for" sea life. Whales, seals, sea lions, and walruses are also important. Paint or draw an underwater scene showing one or more of these animals in its natural habitat.

V. Evaluation

Complete the "Alaska Check-Up" worksheet.

ALASKA

Check•Up

Find the words in the puzzle to fill in the blanks in the sentences below.
You will find the words across, up, and down.

F	O	R	G	E	T	M	E	N	O	T	A	M
W	C	O	N	G	R	E	S	S	B	C	D	T
A	G	R	I	C	U	L	T	U	R	E	X	M
L	O	G	G	I	N	G	E	F	G	S	H	C
R	T	H	E	L	A	S	T	I	J	K	L	K
U	F	R	O	N	T	I	E	R	M	I	N	I
S	A	L	E	U	T	S	O	P	Q	M	R	N
W	I	L	L	O	W	T	S	U	V	O	W	L
P	T	A	R	M	I	G	A	N	X	S	Y	E
F	O	R	T	Y	N	I	N	T	H	Z	A	Y
I	N	D	I	A	N	S	B	C	D	E	F	G

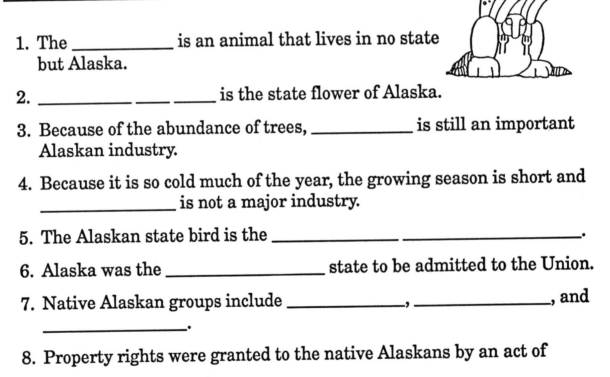

1. The _____ is an animal that lives in no state
   but Alaska.

2. _____ ____ ____ is the state flower of Alaska.

3. Because of the abundance of trees, _____ is still an important
   Alaskan industry.

4. Because it is so cold much of the year, the growing season is short and
   _____ is not a major industry.

5. The Alaskan state bird is the _____ _____.

6. Alaska was the _____ state to be admitted to the Union.

7. Native Alaskan groups include _____, _____, and
   _____.

8. Property rights were granted to the native Alaskans by an act of
   _____.

9. The nickname for Alaska is _____ _____ _____.

HAWAII

The Aloha State

Kukui

Nene (Hawaiian Goose)

Hibiscus

223

HAWAII

Fact • Sheet

FAST FACTS

1. **CAPITAL:** Honolulu

2. **BORDERING STATES:** None

3. **THREE MAJOR CITIES:** Honolulu • Hilo • Kahului

4. **ADMITTED TO UNION:** August 21, 1959

OTHER INTERESTING FACTS:

1. Hawaii was the fiftieth (and final) state to be admitted to the Union.

2. The Hawaiian population is a varied and colorful one. Since the Polynesians arrived in their huge canoes more than a thousand years ago, people have flocked to this paradise-like setting from all parts of the world. The rich blend of beliefs, habits, and traditions have resulted in Hawaii's diverse culture and lifestyles.

3. The Hawaiian Islands were formed by volcanic eruptions that took place over millions of years. They are actually composed of hard lava that in many areas has been worn down into soft, fertile soil. This soil provides rich farmlands for growing coffee, pineapple, sugarcane, and other crops.

SUPER FACT: *Did you know* that Kauai's Mount Waialeale is one of the most rainy spots in the world? It receives an average of 460 inches of rain a year!

Unit•At•A•Glance

Read and complete all activities, beginning with **I** and ending with **V**.

I. Language

Legends have played an important role in the history and development of Hawaii. Write your own original legend about the formation of the Hawaiian Islands.

II. Environmental Studies

Compare and contrast the importance of agricultural products of Hawaii with those of your own state. List the leading products of both states and place them in rank order of importance.

III. Math

Interview five people to find out how many can (1) correctly spell the word Hawaii on the first try, (2) name the date the state was admitted to the Union, and (3) name the state capital. Graph your findings to determine how "Hawaii smart" your friends are.

IV. Enrichment

Make up a dance or a chant to express and preserve an ethnic tradition as did the early Hawaiians. Plan a luau complete with an ethnic menu to celebrate tradition.

V. Evaluation

Complete the "Hawaii Check-Up" worksheet.

HAWAII

Make a picture dictionary for a non-English speaking visitor to Hawaii. Include recreation, occupations, agricultural products, scenic sites, the state's symbols, and other facts and information to help the visitor enjoy the Hawaiian visit.

Teacher's Toolbox

U.S. MAP WITH STATES AND CAPITALS

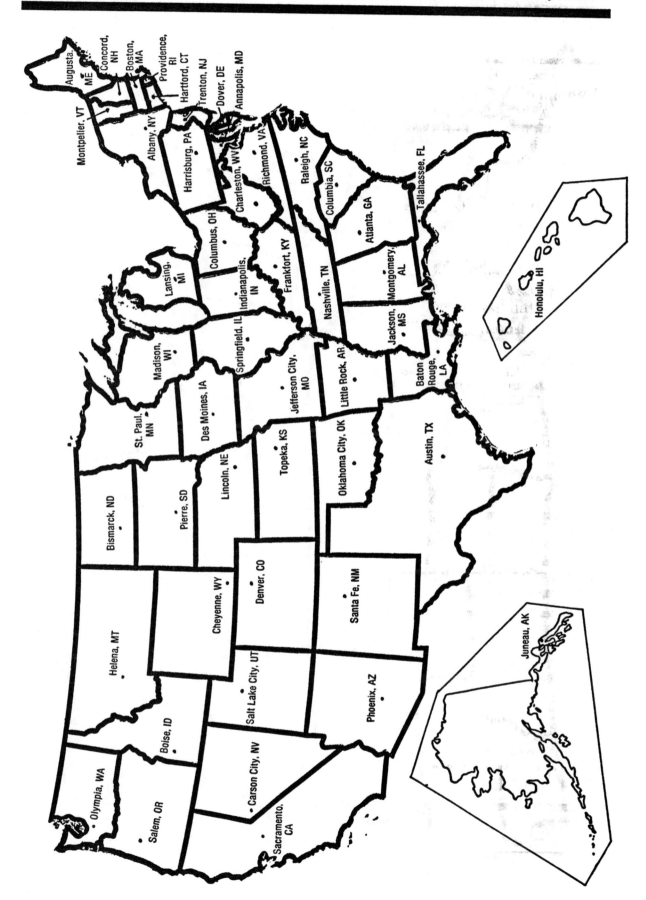

OUTLINE MAP OF THE UNITED STATES

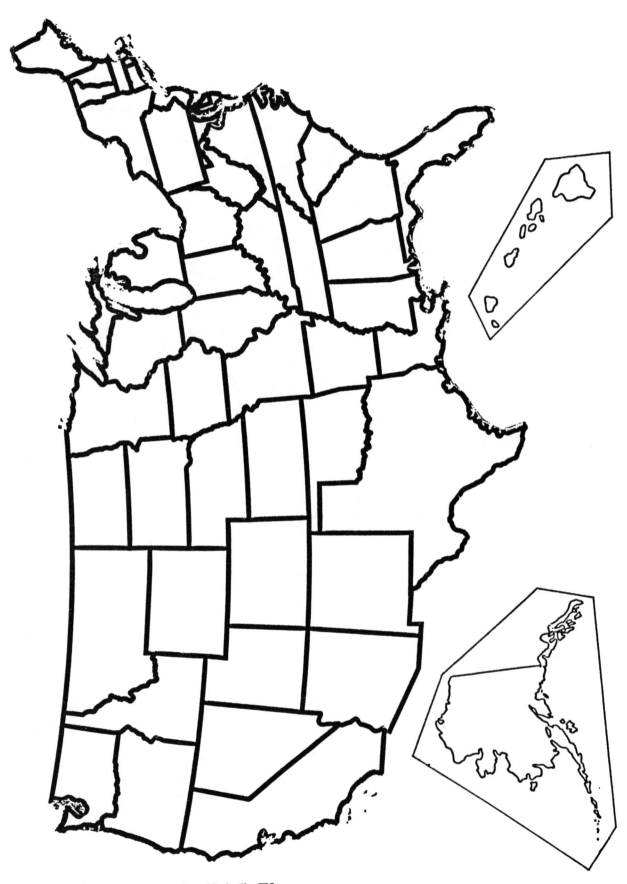

THE CAPITAL

Washington, D.C.

Washington, D.C., is the only American city that is not part of a state. It covers an area of land called the District of Columbia. There is no large industry in the city because it is the headquarters of the United States government—government is this city's business!

Washington is one of the few cities whose design was completely planned before construction began. George Washington hired Pierre Charles L'Enfant, a French engineer, to design its layout. In 1800, Washington replaced Philadelphia as our nation's capital.

Imagine you are planning a trip to Washington, D.C. First determine how many miles it is from your hometown by consulting a map with a distance key. Imagine you will tour the beautiful west-central part of the city, with its green lawns, white marble buildings, and famous monuments. Write down how you think you will feel or what you think you will do when you see each of the famous attractions listed below.

EXAMPLE: Lincoln Memorial *I will hold up a penny so I can compare the tiny image of Lincoln with the huge monument.*

Vietnam War Memorial_____ Wright Brothers' airplane_____

_____ _____

_____ _____

Washington Monument_____ The White House _____

_____ _____

_____ _____

Smithsonian Museum _____ U.S. Constitution _____

_____ _____

_____ _____

Hope Diamond_____ Jefferson Memorial _____

_____ _____

_____ _____

Name_____

STARS AND STRIPES FOREVER

American Flag Crossword Puzzle

Even though many people still think that Betsy Ross made the first United States flag, it is now believed by most historians that this story is simply a legend. Betsy Ross, a seamstress, did make many flags during the Revolutionary War, but no one knows for sure who made the *first* flag.

To learn more about the rich and colorful history of the American flag, solve the American Flag Crossword Puzzle below.

ACROSS
1. The stripes in the flag stand for the thirteen original _____.
2. The national anthem is call the *Star-Spangled* _____.
3. U.S. citizens may show respect to the flag by giving the *Pledge of* _____.
4. The flag flies over the Capitol in Washington, D.C., every _____.
5. In 1818, Congress decided that the national flag would be made of thirteen stripes, with a star for each _____.
6. The most popular name for the American flag is the *Stars and* _____.

DOWN
1. A flag flown at half-mast is a sign of _____.
2, 7, and 5. The American flag's colors are _____, _____, and _____.
3. The flag is usually displayed outdoors between sunrise and _____.
4. A man or woman in military uniform will _____ the flag as it passes.
6. In 1814, Francis Scott _____ wrote the poem that became the national anthem.

Name_____

PRESENTING THE PRESIDENTS

Names of United States Presidents through 1992

President	Birth State	Political Party	Dates Served
George Washington	Virginia	None	1789–1797
John Adams	Massachusetts	Federalist	1797–1801
Thomas Jefferson	Virginia	Democratic-Republican	1801–1809
James Madison	Virginia	Democratic-Republican	1809–1817
James Monroe	Virginia	Democratic-Republican	1817–1825
John Quincy Adams	Massachusetts	Democratic-Republican	1825–1829
Andrew Jackson	South Carolina	Democratic	1829–1837
Martin Van Buren	New York	Democratic	1837–1841
William H. Harrison	Virginia	Whig	1841
John Tyler	Virginia	Whig	1841–1845
James K. Polk	North Carolina	Democratic	1845–1849
Zachary Taylor	Virginia	Whig	1849–1850
Millard Fillmore	New York	Whig	1850–1853
Franklin Pierce	New Hampshire	Democratic	1853–1857
James Buchanan	Pennsylvania	Democratic	1857–1861
Abraham Lincoln	Kentucky	Republican	1861–1865
Andrew Johnson	North Carolina	National Union	1865–1869
Ulysses S. Grant	Ohio	Republican	1869–1877
Rutherford B. Hayes	Ohio	Republican	1877–1881
James A. Garfield	Ohio	Republican	1881

President	Birth State	Political Party	Dates Served
Chester A. Arthur	Vermont	Republican	1881–1885
Grover Cleveland	New Jersey	Democratic	1885–1889
Benjamin Harrison	Ohio	Republican	1889–1893
Grover Cleveland	New Jersey	Democratic	1893–1897
William McKinley	Ohio	Republican	1897–1901
Theodore Roosevelt	New York	Republican	1901–1909
William H. Taft	Ohio	Republican	1909–1913
Woodrow Wilson	Virginia	Democratic	1913–1921
Warren G. Harding	Ohio	Republican	1921–1923
Calvin Coolidge	Vermont	Republican	1923–1929
Herbert C. Hoover	Iowa	Republican	1929–1933
Franklin D. Roosevelt	New York	Democratic	1933–1945
Harry S. Truman	Missouri	Democratic	1945–1953
Dwight D. Eisenhower	Texas	Republican	1953–1961
John F. Kennedy	Massachusetts	Democratic	1961–1963
Lyndon B. Johnson	Texas	Democratic	1963–1969
Richard M. Nixon	California	Republican	1969–1974
Gerald R. Ford	Nebraska	Republican	1974–1977
Jimmy Carter	Georgia	Democratic	1977–1981
Ronald W. Reagan	Illinois	Republican	1981–1989
George H. W. Bush	Massachusetts	Republican	1989–1992
Bill Clinton	Arkansas	Democratic	1992–

PARK PLACES

Listing Of National Parks

PARK	LOCATION	PARK	LOCATION
Acadia	Maine	Isle Royale	Michigan
American Samoa	American Samoa	Katmai	Alaska
Arches	Utah	Kenai Fjords	Alaska
Badlands	South Dakota	Kings Canyon	California
Big Bend	Texas	Kobuk Valley	Alaska
Biscayne	Florida	Lake Clark	Alaska
Bryce Canyon	Utah	Lassen Volcanic	California
Canyonlands	Utah	Mammoth Cave	Kentucky
Capitol Reef	Utah	Mesa Verde	Colorado
Carlsbad Caverns	New Mexico	Mount Rainier	Washington
Channel Islands	California	North Cascades	Washington
Crater Lake	Oregon	Olympic	Washington
Denali	Alaska	Petrified Forest	Arizona
Everglades	Florida	Redwood	California
Gates of the Arctic	Alaska	Rocky Mountain	Colorado
Glacier	Montana	Sequoia	California
Glacier Bay	Alaska	Shenandoah	Virginia
Grand Canyon	Arizona	Theodore Roosevelt	North Dakota
Grand Teton	Wyoming	Virgin Islands	Virgin Islands
Great Basin	Nevada	Voyageurs	Minnesota
Great Smoky Mts.	North Carolina, Tennessee	Wind Cave	South Dakota
Guadalupe Mountains	Texas	Wrangell-St. Elias	Alaska
Haleakala	Hawaii	Yellowstone	Idaho, Montana, Wyoming
Hawaii Volcanoes	Hawaii	Yosemite	California
Hot Springs	Arkansas	Zion	Utah

ANSWER PLEASE

Answers for Puzzles and Quizzes

Page 18
1. sandworms
2. Chickadee
3. Augusta
4. Evergreens, leafy trees
5. Logging
6. Portland
7. herring, cod, scallops
8. clams
9. California

Page 22
1. Freedom Trail
2. Harvard
3. Cape Cod
4. Mayflower
5. Bay State
6. basketball
7. Plymouth
8. Boston, Springfield
9. Chickadee
10. dollar bills

Page 48
populated, apart, residents, farms, forests, produce, Atlantic City, The Garden State, purple violet, Eastern Gold Finch, Red Oak, diverse

Page 74
1. the Cherokee Rose
2. the Brown Thrasher
3. Atlanta
4. Columbus, Savannah

Page 112
1. O
2. O
3. X
4. X
5. O
6. X
7. O
8. X
9. X
10. O
11. X

Page 98

Page 116

ANSWER PLEASE

Answers for Puzzles and Quizzes

Page 182

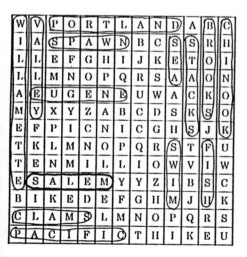

Page 222

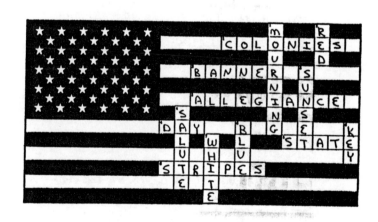

Page 186
1. Italy (TYLAI), Georgia (GRIAOGE), Alaska (KSLAAA), Vermont (TMNREVO)
2. potatoes (STATPEOO), barley (YLERAB),
3. gem (MGE)
4. Syringa (RSGAYIN)
5. Idaho Falls (AHDOI SLAFL)
6. Washington (SHAWGTNINO), Utah (HUAT)
7. logging (GOLNIGG), mining (GNIMNI)
8. Mountain Bluebird (TANNOUMI BERDULBI)

Page 232

Page 212

INDEX

Please consult Table of Contents to find location of activity page (**Unit At A Glance**) and evaluation page (**Check-Up**) for each state. Each **Unit At A Glance** page contains activities, lessons, and projects in the areas of **Language, Math, Environmental Studies, and Enrichment.**

INDEX